S~~KIPPING~~

to SCHOOL

SKIPPING
to SCHOOL

*Memories of a Liverpool
Girlhood 1937–1948*

Doris Calder

The
History
Press

To my father George, my mother Alice, and my sister Joyce.

Thanks for the memories.

Cover illustration © Getty Images

First published 2013

The History Press
The Mill, Brimscombe Port
Stroud, Gloucestershire, GL5 2QG
www.thehistorypress.co.uk

British Library Cataloguing in Publication Data.
A catalogue record for this book is available from the British Library.

ISBN 978 0 7524 9154 7

Typesetting and origination by The History Press
Printed in Great Britain

CONTENTS

	About the Author	6
	Acknowledgement	6
Chapter One	Skipping to School	7
Chapter Two	School Rules	10
Chapter Three	The School Year	17
Chapter Four	Pills, Potions and Childhood Illnesses	26
Chapter Five	My Friends and the Games We Played	35
Chapter Six	Holidays	58
Chapter Seven	Parties and Presents	74
Chapter Eight	My Mother	88
Chapter Nine	My Father	119
Chapter Ten	Wartime Experiences	131
Chapter Eleven	Make-do-and-Mend	154
Chapter Twelve	The Lights Come on Again	168
Chapter Thirteen	Cycling to School	175

ABOUT THE AUTHOR

The author, in her eighty-second year at the time of writing, still enjoys travelling, visiting places of interest, motoring, sewing, family history, a spot of gardening, going to auction sales and collecting antiques. She holds a BA (Hons) degree in Art and Literature, and a diploma in European Humanities.

ACKNOWLEDGEMENT

Thanks to my son Martin, for his patience and encouragement. Having heard the stories often enough, he told me to write them down.

Chapter One

SKIPPING TO SCHOOL

The summers of the 1930s were quite exceptional. This is not the misty-eyed imaginings of an adult looking back on a well-remembered childhood, but a matter of recorded meteorological fact. The days were hot and sunny, and the nights were warm and still. People kept their doors open long after dark, to let a breeze waft through their houses, keeping them cool throughout the evening. Neighbours chatted over garden fences and walls, couples strolled by, some coming home from a drink at their local, some returning from a visit to friends, others just enjoying an evening walk.

The summers of my childhood were happy times. A carefree season, it was a pause before September brought changes. As summer drew to a close and the season turned, new things happened to me. September of 1937 brought the biggest change in my life so far – I started school. I'd had my fifth birthday in February of that year, and since then I had been waiting to join my older sister at Arnot Street Infants & Juniors School. She was two years older than me and two years ahead at school. The year that I started in the infants she moved up to the juniors, and so I hardly saw her at school after all.

It had been a long wait for me to start school. In the months following my fifth birthday, I watched from our front window as children passed by on their way to school. Arnot Street was only a few minutes' walk away, so I saw the schoolchildren in the morning, at lunchtime and going home in the afternoon. I heard them laughing and talking and I sensed their excitement. I couldn't wait to join them.

Most of the older children walked to school on their own, but the younger children were taken by their mothers. The mothers were happy to walk their children to school in the morning and collect them in the afternoon; it was a chance for them to meet up with other women, have a chat and exchange any news and gossip. In those days, married women with school-age children very rarely went out to work and so could easily fit the school walk around domestic tasks.

Girls and boys did very different things on their way to school. Some of the girls skipped happily, some played avoiding-the-lines-between-the-paving-stones, some just walked, talking and giggling with their friends, while others chased a wooden hoop with a stick. The boys shouted a lot as they played tick, raced each other or ran about, kicking a ball. When September came and I finally started school, it was my turn to skip along and play avoiding-the-lines-between-the-paving-stones. To step on a line meant we could bring a terrible disaster down on our family. Sometimes we would step on a line for a dare, and then flew home to make sure everything was all right.

The first Christmas after starting school, at the top of my list of presents was a new skipping rope. I wanted one of the luxury versions – the Rolls-Royce of skipping ropes – with handles made of light-coloured varnished wood and a top which unscrewed so that the length of the rope could be adjusted. The best feature was the two steel rings holding ball bearings set into the top of the handles, allowing the rope to swivel round smoothly as I skipped. With my deluxe skipping rope, I could now skip to school along with the other children. The more you skipped, the more complicated skipping became. Experienced skippers could perform difficult manoeuvres, such as crossed-hands and whizzing-the-rope-round-at-double-speed (turning it twice for one jump), but only the ball-bearing ropes could be used to do cross-overs.

Chapter Two

SCHOOL RULES

Each day, the school bell rang at ten to nine and twenty past one, giving the signal that the morning or afternoon sessions were about to start and we should all be in school. The bell was housed in an open tower at one end of the building and when the caretaker pulled the rope, it could be heard from a long way off. Once the bell started to ring, the pace of the children suddenly quickened, as they realised time was running out. Skipping ropes were wound up, balls picked up, and any stragglers started to run. No one wanted to miss the line-up in the schoolyard or to be marked late. I was never marked late; I was so keen to get to school and was truly happy when I was there.

The children in each year were split into four classes of about thirty pupils. Each class had a team leader, and each wore a sash in one of the primary colours – red, yellow, green or blue – so we could see who they were. When the handbell was rung, we lined up in the schoolyard behind our own team leader; smallest at the front, tallest at the back. We stayed in our colour teams for games, spelling bees and arithmetic tests. Points were awarded to each team for various achievements. We took great pride in our team and tried our very best to make sure we won one of the awards, either a cup or a shield, which were presented at the end of each school year.

When we'd all managed to line up in silence, without too much pushing and shoving, the whistle blew and we marched into the cloakroom, still in silence, then we hung our outdoor clothes on our own numbered pegs, which we had been given at the start of the year and that were ours for the rest of the year.

In the classroom we stood by our places in silence until our teacher, Miss Smith, gave us permission to sit. The desks were in pairs, each consisting of a wrought-iron frame, holding two wooden desks with lids and a tip-up bench. Each desk had a china inkwell set into the corner and a long narrow groove for pens, pencils, rulers and rubbers. Miss Smith was a sprightly mature lady, with grey, neatly permed hair, prominent teeth and sharp, bright eyes behind sparkling glasses. Her eyes never missed anything, good or bad. All of the teachers in our infants and juniors school were female and unmarried. Miss Smith took our class for every lesson, except games and art.

At the beginning of every morning and afternoon, the register was duly taken, and woe betide anyone who failed to answer to their name with the correct reply:

'Doris Hinchliffe?'

'Present, Miss Smith.'

Before lessons started in the morning, we had to spend time learning our multiplication tables, and then recite them all together as a class. Every afternoon began with a spelling bee. We were given a slip of lined paper and we wrote down the words that Miss Smith read out. When we'd finished, we swapped it with our neighbour to mark, in order to prevent cheating. We also had sessions when Miss Smith would shoot out random questions to us, on either mental arithmetic or general knowledge.

Good work in general, good behaviour in lessons and punctuality were all rewarded with gold or silver stick-on stars, which were stuck in our exercise books.

◆:◆:◆

Arnot Street School was housed in a typical Victorian building, with shiny red facing bricks at the front, grey common bricks at the back, and brown stone mullions around the windows and doors. The date '1884' was carved on a stone plaque set into the front wall. In the archways over the main doors, clearly carved into the stone, were the words 'Infants' and 'Juniors'.

Inside the school, the classrooms were linked by a series of heavy, dark brown sliding wooden screens. Glass panels were set into the screens just above our head height, so that the teachers could see between the classrooms but the children could not. The school caretaker took tremendous pride in 'his' school, and kept the wooden screens highly polished and shiny. The room always smelt of wood, polish and warm bodies.

Each classroom had a huge fireplace surrounded by a brass and wire-mesh fireguard for safety. Extra heating came from black cast-iron radiators, which were fed by thick black pipes that looked like drainpipes. In winter, the caretaker came in very early before school started to stoke the coal boilers, which fed hot water to the radiators, and he filled the metal hoppers with coal. He put one hopper in each fireplace in the morning, and at intervals throughout the day he came round the classrooms to feed the fires with coal – he kept a good blaze going all day. In winter, school was a cosy place to be; some of the children were probably warmer at school than they would have been at home.

The toilets were across the schoolyard, close to the wall which backed onto the railway line. They were in two separate blocks – one block for girls and one block for boys – and each block contained five individual toilets. The girls' block had large wooden seats with a hole in the middle and white porcelain toilet basins underneath. The wooden doors had deep gaps at the top and bottom, and old iron latches that didn't work very well, due to years of use. In summer, the biggest problem was stopping the boys from peeping under the doors. In winter, the worst problem was the cold; we had to wrap up in our coats and put on our woolly gloves to go 'across the yard'. When it was pouring with rain and the wind was howling, we had to struggle to sit on the seats and keep the doors closed at the same time.

We were never allowed out of lessons to go to the toilet; we could only go at break times or lunchtime. Occasionally, children who'd tried desperately hard to put off going until break time, lunchtime or home time, had an accident. If by any chance someone had diarrhoea, we all knew about it. After all this time, I still remember the name of the girl who was sitting next to me when she had a severe bout of diarrhoea. We all had to leave the room while the caretaker threw sawdust on the floor, before he cleaned up the area with disinfectant.

◆❖◆

In winter when it snowed, before school and during breaks, the playground rang with shouts, laughter and squeals of delight, as the boys pushed snow down the back of each other's collars and chased the girls with snowballs. The boys made slides wherever there was a good patch of smooth ice. When we trooped back into the classroom, our woolly gloves were sopping wet and our hands were red with a cold we never seemed to feel. Underneath our thick brown woolly stockings, most of the girls had wet knickers and bruised bottoms from whizzing along and falling on the slides started by the boys. Sometimes we tore holes in our stockings and scraped our knees. In the warmth of the classroom, our eyes sparkled and our cheeks glowed. Life was fun. Later, when we realised what we'd done, we dreaded going home to face our mothers. Once school was over, we couldn't wait to get out into the snow again. At that age I could never understand why adults groaned when snow appeared and why they thought it was only pretty on Christmas cards.

❖

On my way to and from school I had to pass what I thought was a very scary animal – I was convinced he was a lion. The beast lived in our neighbours' house, next door but one. The 'lion' had a thick, fluffy golden-brown coat, which stood up around his head like a mane. The strangest thing about him was his deep-purple tongue lolling out of his mouth as he sat with his big paws hanging over the edge of the front step.

I eyed him nervously as I walked past, torn between slowing down to look and speeding up to get by safely. The 'lion' never roared, but watched me silently. I told my mother how concerned I was about the lion that lived in our neighbours' house. She said I was not to be so silly, that it was not a lion but a chow-chow, a pedigree dog from China, and his name was Chang. I was never really convinced that this was true.

I breathed a sigh of relief when one day the dog was no longer in the doorway. I thought he'd died. After a couple of weeks, the dog suddenly re-appeared looking very sorry for himself. I found out he'd been for an operation to fix his ingrowing eyelashes, apparently a common problem with the chow-chows, and his eyes were swollen and some of the fur around them had been cut away. In the end, I felt sorry for him; he never ran about freely or chased a ball like other dogs. His owners were an elderly couple, Mr and Mrs Ellams. Mr Ellams was pale and sickly and didn't work, and Mrs Ellams was small and plump with a red face, and they didn't have any children. The exotic, purple-tongued dog was the centre of their lives; they fed him on the best of food and wouldn't allow anyone else to stroke or walk him. Some of the children in my street who didn't have a dog organised a dog-walking group, but Chang was one dog they had to leave alone.

◆:◆

Children who lived near enough to school could go home for lunch if they wanted. For those who lived too far away and didn't have time to go home, school dinners were provided, delivered daily by a van, in heated metal containers.

During morning and afternoon breaks, we all had milk given out by the milk monitors, at a small cost of tuppence ha'penny a bottle (about one new penny). Being the milk monitor was an important job, given to those juniors in their final year who had performed well in their tests and had a good attendance record. The monitors wore blue and gold badges. The small milk bottles came in crates of twelve, each bottle had a cardboard top with a round hole marked in the middle, through which we pushed our fingers and inserted a waxed paper straw.

In the Summer Term of my last year in the juniors, as a reward for my academic achievements and good attendance, I became a milk monitor. I felt so important wearing my blue and gold milk monitor's badge; I must have been insufferable for the whole term.

Chapter Three

THE SCHOOL YEAR

I started school just in time for Harvest Festival, the first big event of the new school year. Local bakers supplied bread made in the shape of golden sheaves of corn, large cottage loaves, twisted circles and long thin plaits. Some loaves were decorated with the name of the school, or the year (1936, 1937 etc.), the figures of which were made by placing strips of dough on top of the loaves before they were baked.

For the Harvest Festival service children were encouraged to bring in fruit or vegetables. Some of the produce was grown by parents, most of it we had to buy, and all of it was English except for the bananas, oranges and lemons. Parents with allotments provided marrows, runner beans, onions, leeks and tomatoes. We had to wash the soil off the vegetables, especially the root vegetables – potatoes, carrots and beetroots – before we took them into school. We had to be particularly careful not to damage the green fern-like tops of the carrots, so that they looked pretty in the display. We had to take care with the beetroots; if the tail was cut off too close to the beetroot or the leaves were cut off too low on the stalk, the beetroot would 'bleed'. The huge Savoy cabbages with their bright green curly leaves, took up lots of space in the display, and they were so fresh that their leaves squeaked when pressed.

The eating apples were English varieties: Cox's Pippins, Worcester Permains, Russets and Granny Smiths, and the varieties of pears were Conference, Comice and Beurre Hardy. Most of the fruit came from orchards in Kent or the Vale of Evesham. We knew from our geography lessons that Kent was known as the 'Garden of England'. The fruits were not perfectly shaped like most of the specimens seen nowadays in supermarkets. They were very tasty and each one had its own distinctive flavour. The produce was carefully arranged on the stage at the front of the school hall for everyone to see at assembly. After assembly, the produce was carried over to the church, which was decorated with big bunches of flowers. Many of the flowers were grown by the children's parents alongside the vegetables on their allotments. The flowers were vividly coloured bunches of dahlias, gladioli, daisies and a few roses, although roses were well past their best by Harvest Festival time. In church we had a service celebrating the bountiful harvest of the earth and we sang the Harvest Festival hymn:

We plough the fields and scatter
The Good seed on the land,
But it is fed and watered
By God's almighty hand;
He sends the snow in winter,
The warmth to swell the grain,
The breezes and the sunshine,
And soft refreshing rain.
(*Trinity Hymnal*, 614)

At the end of the service, we said a prayer of thanksgiving. Afterwards, the display was dismantled and the produce was taken away to be distributed to the elderly, the poor and the sick in the neighbourhood, and the flowers were taken to the local hospital.

Once Harvest Festival was over, the next event in the school calendar we had to look forward to was the nativity play in December. Preparations for the play began towards the end of November, when children were chosen to play the main parts: Mary, Joseph, the Three Wise Men, the Shepherds and the Angel Gabriel. We had a manger and doll in store and every year they were brought out, cleaned and refurbished if necessary, ready for the play. I was always picked to play the part of the Angel Gabriel because of my bright gold hair and blue eyes.

My costume was a white sheet, with a hole cut in it for my head and a magnificent pair of wings made from a wire frame covered with white crêpe paper, with dozens and dozens of silver paper shapes stuck onto it which looked like feathers. On my head I wore a gleaming halo made from bright, glittery, gold ribbon wrapped around millinery wire. Being an angel seemed to me to be too goody-goody. I longed to be something more interesting like a shepherd, to paint my face brown, wear a large black moustache, a black wig and a brightly coloured striped cloak. I never got the chance, because of my colouring I was typecast as the Angel Gabriel, much to the amusement of my parents, who saw me in quite a different light.

Every year as a child, at some point during the winter months, I developed tonsillitis. One year I caught it at the beginning of December, just in time, I thought, to get out of playing the part of the angel. No such luck! I wasn't off ill for long enough and when I returned to school, the white sheet, the crêpe paper wings and the golden halo were waiting for me. With my voice now back in good working order, as the curtains parted, once again I stepped forward, held up my arms, opened my wings wide, and gave my familiar speech:

> Fear not, for behold, I bring you glad tidings of great joy,
> Which shall be to all people.
> For unto you a boy is born this day in the city of David a Saviour,
> Which is Christ the Lord.
> (*Luke*, 2:10-11)

I hated the dark nights of winter. After Christmas, it was the long haul through the rest of winter until spring arrived. The clocks went forward an hour at the end of March and the evenings grew lighter by a cock-stride every night. Daffodils came into bloom, and birds would sing noisily as they built their nests. Easter was the first date on the calendar that showed that spring had really arrived.

Easter meant we had two weeks' holiday. We could usually play outside in the Easter holidays; the weather was growing warmer and the sun had lost its winter harshness. I really looked forward to chocolate Easter Eggs. We were not allowed to eat many sweets because they were considered bad for our teeth, so Easter Eggs were a real treat. I was usually given three eggs: one from my mother; one from my father and one from my godmother Auntie Liz, my mother's sister. Chocolate eggs came in many varieties and sizes. Some were wrapped in brightly coloured silver paper, some had our names or 'Happy Easter' piped on in white icing; some had extra packets of chocolates rattling tantalisingly inside and others were beautifully decorated with coloured flowers, fashioned from sweet fondant icing.

There were two shops in particular where we went to see the most amazing displays of chocolate confections. One was Mr Edwards' sweet shop in Aintree, near to where my Auntie Elsie lived. The other was Matti & Tissot in Southport. The shops were very different in style, but they each set out lavish window displays of chocolates for Christmas and Easter. Children and adults were captivated by the wonderful sweet things on display in their windows.

Mr Edwards' shop was in the middle of a small row of shops set back off the main road and used mainly by local people. His window display was lit up with fairy lights and had lots of chocolate eggs with 'Happy Easter' written on in coloured icing, some were even decorated with small roses created from fondant icing and crystallised violet petals. The centrepiece of Mr Edwards' display was a large chocolate windmill. It was on show every year and had sails made from sheets of spun sugar, and there was a small electric motor inside the chocolate windmill, which made the sugar sails turn round slowly. Small windows in the windmill were lit from inside by a tiny coloured light. The windmill was surrounded by eggs made from spun sugar, and the fronts of the eggs were partially cut away to show miniature cardboard figures inside. Mr Edwards also sold eggs made by the mainstream chocolate manufacturers, Cadbury, Rowntree's and Fry's.

Every Easter would see the start to Mr Edwards selling his famous water ices. Triangular in shape, like Toblerones, the ices and had very strong fruity flavours which seemed to explode in the mouth, leaving a tingling sensation like sherbet on the tongue.

The Easter display in the window of Matti & Tissot's shop in Southport was quite different, however. Owned by a Swiss family, Matti & Tissot was a luscious chocolate shop, patisserie and tearoom in the famous arcade of shops along Lord Street. The front window of the shop was set back at an angle from the pavement. The shelves in the shop window were draped with golden yellow satin, and the variety of chocolate items sitting on the shelves and the floor of the window were amazing. There were life-sized chocolate animals – boxing hares, rabbits, roosters, hens sitting in large chocolate baskets, chickens of different sizes and so many beautifully decorated Easter eggs, all made from chocolate and marzipan. It was almost impossible to take it all in!

My sister and I walked from side to side in front of the window of the shop to make sure we saw everything. At the front of the display, wrapped in cellophane paper and tied with silk ribbon, were tiny chocolate eggs and sugared almonds, tucked into china ornaments. Fluffy, yellow baby chicks sat in small baskets, made entirely from marzipan; towards the back of the display stood the larger creations and some enormous chocolate eggs. We wondered how it was possible to make such big, complicated things out of chocolate, and how long it would take to eat such big eggs! Some of the chocolate wonders in the window, especially the larger ones, were not for sale – they were for display only and would be given to the local children's hospital on Easter Sunday.

As we walked into the shop our noses were hit by the tantalising smell of chocolate, and the array of handmade chocolates of all different shapes and sizes set out on small golden trays behind the large glass counter made our eyes shine with wonder. A separate glass counter displayed a selection of luscious cakes and pastries. As a special treat, we went through the shop then down the steps at the back into the tearoom, to have cakes and a pot of tea.

My sister and I always had new shoes for Easter. They were given to us on Easter Sunday morning and we would wear them for the first time to Sunday school. I loved the smell of new leather. Whenever I got new shoes, before I put them on, I poked my nose inside and breathed in deeply to inhale the smell of the leather. What I really longed for was a pair of black patent leather shoes. One Easter, my mother finally decided I could have a pair. I couldn't believe it! I had wanted them for so long. New shoes meant a trip to Hendersons, one of the big department stores in the city centre, where one of my mother's old school friends worked in the shoe department.

I am flat-footed and so I had to be fitted for Kilte shoes, which were specially made for children with flat feet. The shoes had an extended shaped heel under the arch of the shoe for support. There was another brand of shoes sold especially for children, called Start-rite. The typical advert for their shoes was a small plump child striding out in a lovely pair of shoes, wearing a blue coat and a bright red hat topped with a large pom-pom. After I'd been measured for the shoes I had to stand in the 'X-ray' machine. It wasn't a real X-ray machine, it was a glass panel strongly lit from underneath, and when I stood on it wearing just my socks I could see the flesh of my feet glowing red around my bones, which showed up very clearly. It was magic! I stood looking down in wonder at the shape of the bones of my feet, so many small bits of bone. It was easy to see whether or not the shoes fitted correctly and whether or not my toes were scrunched up and if there was enough room for growth. A new pair of Kilte black patent leather shoes was decided upon. The shoes sat in a box in my wardrobe, waiting for Easter Sunday. I opened and closed the box many times, just to make sure I wasn't dreaming.

On Sundays, and other special occasions, my sister and I used to take turns wearing a small fur scarf called a tippet, made of white ermine, which, our mother explained to us, is the winter coat of the stoat. The tippet had small black tails hanging along its body, at one end was the head of the animal with shiny black glass beady eyes while at the other end were four small black and white tails. A clip behind the animal's nose held the head to the tail. The tippet was lined with white satin which felt luxurious against our necks.

Before her marriage, my mother had trained as a furrier and we had lots of small pieces of fur in the house: coney (rabbit), moleskin, musquash and squirrel. Occasionally, as a favour for friends, she would alter or shorten a fur coat for them. She would clean a fur coat by rubbing it with a mixture of warm silver sand and benzine. She kept the bits of fur which were left over from the alterations and used them as trimmings for our coat collars, hats and the backs of mittens.

My Uncle Bill, who was in the Merchant Navy, came home after one of his trips to Canada with a bag of grey squirrel pelts, which my mother made into a stylish, short fur cape lined with grey satin, for his daughter Betty.

After Easter, the next event in the calendar was May Day. We celebrated May Day in school by dancing around a maypole – tying coloured ribbons onto a large pole in the centre of the playground and performing a ritual dance around it. We learnt the intricate system of crossing and weaving the ribbons round the pole, to make a pattern, and then we reversed the process to undo the ribbons.

Empire Day was held on 24th May. All the children who were in the Brownies, Guides, Cubs, Scouts or Boys' Brigade came to school in their uniforms. We saluted the Union Jack, said a prayer and sang some hymns to celebrate the British Empire and its achievements. Large maps of the world were unrolled and hung on the blackboard, showing the Empire coloured in pink stretching all the way around the world. Empire Day was rounded off by a parade around the school playground.

By the time the summer term drew to a close we were ready for the holidays. Reports were sent home in a sealed envelope with a small tear-off slip to be returned by our parents. I was nearly always top of the class, but one year, 1943, to my shame, I came fourth! I still have this report to remind me of my fall from grace.

Chapter Four

PILLS, POTIONS AND CHILDHOOD ILLNESSES

Before I started school, I'd already caught measles and chickenpox, which my sister contracted at school and gave to me at home. Measles seemed to be the most dangerous, as the doctor came to visit me twice. He took my temperature several times then gave my mother some foul-tasting medicine for me to take. This was in the days before penicillin was available. I knew I was very ill, because I had to stay in bed for a week with the curtains drawn to protect my eyes from bright light, and the fire in my bedroom was lit continuously. Things had to be serious for me to be allowed a fire in my bedroom; even when it was so cold that we could see our breath on the way upstairs, we were not allowed to have a fire in our bedrooms.

In winter, going upstairs to bed meant dressing in long winceyette nightdresses and warm woolly bed socks. On the way upstairs, we had either a metal or a stone hot water bottle, clutched tightly under one arm. If we were lucky, the oven shelves in the kitchen range would still be warm from cooking and we wrapped them up in a piece of sheeting to take upstairs and put in our beds. Our soft feather beds, with their warm winter flannelette sheets and pretty flower-patterned eiderdowns, were nice and cosy once we'd snuggled down under the covers.

To keep us warm during the day, we wore Chilprufe Liberty bodices over our vests. They were thick white cotton sleeveless vests, like waistcoats, strengthened with white tape and fastened up the front with small, cotton covered metal buttons.

When summer came, the flannelette bed sheets were replaced with cotton sheets, and the eiderdown by a fine white cotton bedspread embroidered with white lovers' knots and flowers. My white cotton nightdress case was embroidered with a matching pattern, and the word 'nightdress' was stitched right across the middle. I still have both of these things.

Most of the children I knew, including school friends and relatives, had all had the childhood illnesses: measles, chickenpox, mumps and whooping cough. It was quite important for the boys to have mumps when they were young, because if they caught it later in life it could make them sterile. I hated chickenpox because of the itching; I scratched and scratched at the rash all over my body and had to have my hands tied up in white cotton gloves, but I still managed to make myself bleed when I picked the scabs. Fortunately, most of the spots were on my body and not on my face, so I didn't have any scars.

After I started school, I caught mumps. This was very uncomfortable as my neck was rubbed with camphorated oil and wrapped in a thick woolly comforter made from one of my father's stump socks (more about these later). I had difficulty eating, swallowing, or speaking for a week. As a child, I was always very talkative (I still am), but when I had mumps I could barely croak, which was a welcome relief to my family.

Sometimes I didn't mind being ill, as my mother wrapped me up in a big fluffy blanket, turned out the lights, drew the settee up to the fire, sat me on her knee and rocked me back and forth while she sang:

Just a song at twilight, when the lights are low;
And the flick'ring shadows softly come and go.
Tho' the heart be weary, sad the day and long,
Still to us at twilight comes love's old song,
Comes love's old sweet song.
(Bingham and Molloy)

The combination of the warm blanket, the gentle rocking and the pictures I saw in the flames dancing in the fireplace soon sent me to sleep. My mother was a firm believer not only in the power of sleep to heal, but also, love, warmth and a good cuddle.

We managed to survive all our childhood ailments and in the process we built up our antibodies, which stood us in good stead as we grew into fit, healthy adults. There were two illnesses which we really feared – diphtheria and polio, which thankfully neither my sister nor I ever caught. Large orange and black notices on hoardings warned us that 'DIPHTHERIA CAN KILL!' A child with diphtheria was often put into the isolation ward in the Fever Hospital, until they were no longer infectious.

The Salk vaccine for polio was still in the early stages of experimentation in America and had not yet been produced for widespread use. A small number of children died, and some who developed polio were left with partial paralysis. Sadly, a few had to spend what remained of their lives confined in an iron lung.

My mother had many good remedies for seeing us through our minor childhood complaints. They were purchased from either Boots the Chemist or from our local chemist, Mr Turnpenny MPS. Inside his shop, one wall was taken up by a brown wooden cabinet which contained dozens of drawers like small boxes. Each box had a small glass knob and bore a white label with the name of the contents written on it in large black letters. In the window were three large glass flasks, each one was filled with a brightly coloured liquid, red, yellow, or blue, but I think they were for decoration only.

Mr Turnpenny stood behind his counter, dressed in a crisp, white cotton coat and a pair of sparkling gold-rimmed glasses. His counter was raised on a step, and customers looked up to Mr Turnpenny in more ways than one. He would walk around his counter and step down to have a closer look at the customer's complaint. He was a fountain of knowledge and knew almost everything about any ailment, and he gave advice on minor complaints, which saved his customers the expense of a visit to the doctor that had to be paid for every visit.

He produced many wonderful concoctions, which we called his 'cure-alls', and every one of his potions was dispensed in a brown glass bottle, which hid the contents from prying eyes. Each bottle bore a label stating Mr Turnpenny's name, the contents, the correct dosage and the date. His own cough mixtures were legendary: red cherry-flavoured syrup for children and a strong potion with an aftertaste of ammonia for adults, both of which were guaranteed to cure.

Customers felt free to discuss their most intimate complaints with him in great detail: bowel movements, piles, problems with their water works, women's problems and boils in unmentionable places, to name but a few. He was a man of great discretion; a secret was safe with him.

Nurse Roan, the District Nurse, was a frequent visitor to Mr Turnpenny's shop. She was a tall stately lady, who always wore a navy blue gabardine coat over her crisp blue and white uniform, and a small navy blue pork pie hat. Her black bicycle had high handlebars, in a style we called 'sit up and beg'. It had a big black box strapped onto the back containing things we could only speculate about. We made very rude guesses about what they could possibly be, and tittered and giggled amongst ourselves. When we were young, the rudest words we could think of saying out loud were 'knickers' and 'District Nurse'.

Nurse Roan was a mystery as she came and went around the neighbourhood on her large black bicycle. Sometimes, after Nurse Roan had been to a house, a baby would appear. We were convinced she either kept them in her black bag, or she bought them from Mr Turnpenny's shop. We didn't believe the tale told to us about the gooseberry bush; I'd looked under the gooseberry bush in my Uncle Harry's garden and I'd never seen a baby under it. I was quite anxious one day when I saw my mother talking to Nurse Roan for a very long time. I didn't fancy a new baby in the house, I enjoyed being the youngest, and babies seemed to cry a lot and take up a lot of time. I watched my mother carefully for a while and waited for the baby to appear, but nothing happened. I was amazed one Sunday to see Nurse Roan in church with her husband and son – she was just a normal human being after all!

Friday nights, after we'd had a bath and our hair had been washed, was the time when my mother brought out and administered her tried and tested remedies. From various large and small brown bottles came an assortment of potions. To keep our bowels regular we had to have a teaspoonful of either Syrup of Senna, or Syrup of Figs, both equally obnoxious. Next, a dessertspoonful of cod liver oil and malt was scooped from a very large bottle – it slipped easily off the spoon, down unwilling throats. The sharp taste of the treacly malt could not disguise the strong fishy aftertaste of the cod liver oil, which came back repeatedly into our mouths. For a high temperature or a slight feverish attack, out came a clear glass bottle containing a colourless liquid called Fenning's Fever Cure; it had a sharp bitter taste and gave a slight burning sensation on the way down, but it did the trick.

The worst remedy I had to take was the dreaded Brimstone and Treacle. Brimstone was another name for sulphur. Every spring I used to break out in large pink lumps, called heat bumps, which were incredibly itchy. To ease the itching, I used to dig my thumbnail deep into each of them to form a cross. These heat bumps were due, apparently, to the overheating of my blood and I had to have doses of Brimstone and Treacle to cool me down and clear out my system. This time the thick dark yellow doses came by the tablespoon from a huge brown jar. I dreaded having to take this mixture, as the smell of sulphur seemed to ooze from every pore in my body. The smell of hydrogen sulphide was appalling when I had wind and went to the toilet, and I desperately hoped no one was around when this happened.

Heat bumps were one thing, I could cope with them, but insect bites were totally different! In a field full of people, all the insects would head straight for me – horseflies, midges, fleas, you name them, they loved to take a bite out of me. The horsefly bites were the most unbearable. The area around the bite would swell into a hard, red, shiny throbbing lump about three inches in diameter, and then it would weep for days. One summer, during the holidays, we went with the school to a farm for a week's camping and pea picking. My feet were so badly bitten by horseflies they had to be bandaged and I couldn't wear my sandals. When my mother saw me being helped off the bus, she thought I'd had an accident – 'What have you done now?' she exclaimed. My vulnerability to insect bites has never gone: a few years ago on holiday in Lake Constance, Germany, I got 147 mosquito bites (yes, I counted them) all over my body and had to be pumped full of cortisone. The German doctor in the local hospital raised his hands in horror and said, 'Ach du meine Güte! Never have I seen such legs!' And he wasn't talking about the shape.

I was a blood donor for fifty years and I was usually bled into a dry bottle because my blood contained an unusual set of antibodies. My blood was used for research. Sometimes I wonder if it was the result of my body trying to protect itself over the years from the continued onslaught by the various insects.

For an upset stomach, we used to take Milk of Magnesia, dispensed from a dark blue glass bottle. The so-called 'milk' was white, gooey, and powdery and clung to our teeth. There was no escape from the administration of these remedies, we just had to grin and bear them. After all this, we would take a smooth white emulsion as a tonic, which was rather pleasant.

We were never allowed to take time off school unless it was absolutely necessary. If we felt a bit off colour in the mornings, we were always told, 'Go to school and if you still don't feel well you can always stay off after you come home for lunch'. We very rarely did! My mother could always tell when we were really ill; any attempt at pretending to be sick or malingering was nipped smartly in the bud.

I seemed to be particularly susceptible to throat infections. When I developed my yearly bout of tonsillitis it wasn't all bad, because the cure recommended by Dr Solomon, our family doctor, included plenty of ice cream to cool my sore throat. I loved ice cream and I could hardly believe my luck! When I was young, doctors were reluctant to have a patient's tonsils removed unless it was really necessary. The operation was considered dangerous, not only for the patient, but also for the doctor doing the operation, as he could catch an infection. As I grew older, the bouts of tonsillitis grew fewer and fewer, and the threat of an operation went away.

Beecham's powders and cinnamon toast were my mother's favourite treatment for a cold, and they always did the trick. On the other hand, my father professed his chosen remedy to be: go to bed, hang your hat on the end of the bed and drink enough whisky to make your hat disappear!

My mother also consulted Dr Solomon about my sweaty feet. My socks were always damp and the linings of my shoes and sandals curled up inside and went crisp. I often had to leave them outside the back door to dry, but he said she would have more to worry about if I didn't perspire at all!

Because we sat so close together and the school was warm, nits were sometimes a problem and were occasionally found on the heads of some children when we were inspected by the school nurse. We used to call her the 'nit nurse'. If anything was found, a very discreet note was sent home. To be found with nits was considered very shameful and a bad reflection on the cleanliness and hygiene in your home. I remember coming home from school one day and telling my mother I'd seen something crawling on the collar of the girl who sat next to me.

My mother was galvanised into action. Derbac soap was needed, the best remedy for nits available at the time. She dashed to school to report the matter, and then flew round to Mr Turnpenny's chemist shop to buy some Derbac. The soap was very dark brown, almost black in colour, and it contained coal tar and smelled very strongly of disinfectant. Armed with this and a fine-toothed steel comb, my mother set to work. I had to sit under a strong light and stay still for what seemed like hours, whilst each strand of hair was carefully inspected for any telltale signs of the minute eggs. Particular attention was given to the area behind my ears, because this apparently was the favourite breeding place for nits. Unfortunately, some were found and for the next few weeks my hair was regularly washed with Derbac soap. My head was sore with the continued search for eggs or any other signs of life. I was sworn to secrecy, no one was to know about the nits. My mother considered it to be a very bad reflection on her. Reeking of Derbac soap, I'm sure anyone who came near me might have guessed though.

Scarlet fever was a serious illness, and though I never caught it, my sister did. It was very infectious and dangerous, with nasty side effects. She had to go into an isolation ward at the Fever Hospital for two weeks. I was not allowed to visit her, and my parents could only see her at first through a glass screen. This was a very worrying time for everyone in the family. Fortunately she made a good recovery.

Chapter Five

MY FRIENDS AND THE GAMES WE PLAYED

When I started school, my friends were no longer confined to cousins and the children of my mother's friends, I met children from other parts of the neighbourhood and I began to make new friends. We gradually settled down into our own groups. We met to walk to school together and played lots of games in the playground at break or outside after school. My group of best friends was Pauline, whose father worked as a caretaker for the Trustee Savings Bank; Evelyn, from a Jewish family who had fled from Austria to escape the Nazis – her mother had a dress shop and her father was a doctor; and Pamela, whose father was in the army. Pamela's father was often away on service and so she and her mother lived with her grandparents.

Ball games were popular. 'Tensy' was a game that involved a series of ten difficult manoeuvres performed with two balls against a wall: underarm, over-arm, between your legs, behind your back and facing away from the wall, if you dropped the ball before the ten tests were done, you had to start all over again. Having mastered Tensy, the more clever ones learnt how to juggle with two balls. We also played 'Piggy in the Middle': two people threw the ball backwards and forwards over the head of a third person, the 'piggy in the middle', who could escape only if she jumped up and caught the ball.

It was a strict rule that we were not allowed to play ball games on Sundays. Sundays were for going to Sunday school, having Sunday dinner at two o'clock and visiting relatives. After dinner on Sunday my father would take the opportunity to have his 'forty winks'. When it was our turn, we visited the family grave in Anfield Cemetery. On Mothering Sunday, at Sunday school, we were each given a scented card to take home to our mothers as a thank you for her loving care throughout the year. The cards were often decorated with roses or violets, along with a picture of a mother and child and a verse from the Bible.

The family took it in turns to take flowers to the family grave in Anfield Cemetery. We bought the flowers on Saturday and took them to the cemetery on Sunday morning, with some fresh cold water carried in a metal hot water bottle, to save the long walk to the cemetery tap. We removed the faded flowers from the marble bowl on the grave and replaced them with carefully arranged fresh ones, putting the old flowers in the wire basket at the corner of the plot. Once we'd done this, we were free to wander round the cemetery, looking at flowers and new wreaths on other graves and reading the inscriptions on some of the elaborately carved gravestones.

Anfield Cemetery is a vast place, light and open, with wide roadways and paths, red sandstone walls and carefully tended grass areas. It was so big you could get lost in it, but so open and relaxed you would never be frightened. It had separate areas for each denomination: Church of England, Roman Catholic, Methodist, Presbyterian, Nonconformist and Jewish, with a Garden of Remembrance for those who chose to be cremated.

There were so many gravestones in different shapes – crosses, books, scrolls, urns and weeping angels – and sizes and materials. Some had small statues of sweet cherubs, in memory of children who had died. The gravestones were carved from different types of stone: red sandstone, grey granite and black or white marble, with gold lettering. A few of the monuments were very grand and surrounded by wrought-iron railings, and we wondered who could afford such splendid gravestones.

On Sunday afternoons, after we'd had our dinner, if we were not going for a walk with our mother, we went with her to visit my aunts. When we were old enough we went on our own. Sometimes we went to visit Uncle Harry, one of my favourite uncles. Visiting relatives on a Sunday was a family ritual. Three of my aunts lived together in a roomy old house with a cellar, which was rumoured to have an entrance to an underground tunnel that led to the sewers and the crypt in the local church. I never saw it and neither did any of my cousins; all I could see was a big stack of coal in the corner. Perhaps it was just a tale to keep us out.

After devouring a huge dinner, the aunts washed the dishes then 'banked up' the fire with slack – this was minute pieces of coal packed tightly together, forming a crust over the fire which kept it burning slowly throughout the afternoon nap. They drew their armchairs up to the fire then fell asleep, snoring thunderously with the occasional snort, so loud that the windows rattled. My cousins, my sister and I had to sit on a large sofa covered with black horsehair, which scratched our legs, and listen to the cacophony of sound. We had to keep quiet and amuse ourselves, stifling our giggles. I thought to myself, 'I hope I never grow so old that I have to take an after dinner nap and snore'. As soon as the snoring aunts woke up, one of them, Auntie Liz, poked the fire vigorously with a brass-handled poker, making it burst into life again and burn with a bright flame. They then set about making tea. Sunday was a ritual of set meals.

At the end of the road where my aunts lived there was a small private dairy called Rushton's. The Rushton's dairy kept a small herd of cows in a field and a couple of pigs in an old pigsty with flagstone walls. Customers could have their milk delivered or go to the dairy with their own jug. One Sunday afternoon, when my aunts ran out of milk, we went up to the dairy for some with a jug. Auntie Elsie told us that one of the pigs had just had a large litter of piglets, and that if we asked nicely, Mrs Rushton would probably let us see them. We all raced up to the dairy, where Mrs Rushton couldn't resist our pleas and allowed us in to see the enormous sow lying down on her side feeding ten tiny piglets, all pink and squealing, trying to feed from their mother at once. We'd never been so close to pigs before. We were very excited and we climbed up onto the rails of the fence to get a better look. We'd been there so long my mother came up to the dairy to find out what we were doing, the tea had gone cold and the aunts were waiting for their milk. The first thing my mother saw when she walked into the yard was a row of bottoms as we all hung over the fence, nearly falling into the pigsty. My mother said she knew it was us, she recognised the Miss Muffet pattern flowers on our knickers. She had sewn them herself.

Games taught us a lot. Diabolo was a game which took skill. The Diabolo was a top in the shape of two inverted cones. The player picked it up on a piece of waxed string that was stretched between two sticks. By stretching and releasing the string, the

Diabolo was set spinning and then tossed into the air, where it spun for a few seconds before it was caught again on the string. Mastering the trick was quite an art. Games like Diabolo helped our hand-eye co-ordination and made us quite dexterous.

Hopscotch was a game that involved chalking numbers on the paving stones on the street outside our houses, and then each player would throw a stone at the numbers in turn, before hopping their way around the stone until they had 'stoned' each one. Neighbours would tell us off, shouting 'Don't you chalk outside my house!' Lord knows why, as the chalk would only stay until the rain washed it away.

We also had organised skipping games, which required a heavy rope about twelve feet long. The rope was stretched across the road, and two girls would hold an end each and turn it slowly. We all lined up to take our turn at running through the rope. One song we sang as we jumped through the rope was:

Once you get in
You can't get out
Unless you touch the ground
Turn right round and shout OXO.

We had to do exactly what it said in the song in order to play the game. When you tripped on the rope, it was your turn to take one of the ends. The game finished only when we were tired, our knees were too badly grazed, or when our mothers called to us to go indoors.

The roads were safe places to play, as there was very little traffic in those days. Horses and carts delivered most household essentials, and I only knew three people who had a car: Mr Turnpenny, the chemist, who had a black Morris; Doctor Solomon, the local GP, drove a black Humber, but the grandest car was the big black Austin Princess, which belonged to Mr Platt. The badge across the boot of this car spelled out 'Princess' in elegant chromium letters. Mr Platt was an alderman and the wealthy uncle of one of my mother's friends. I wasn't sure what alderman meant, but he must have been quite important, judging by the size of his car. The rear compartment was separated from the chauffeur and the front passenger space by a sliding glass partition. The car had tip-up seats which meant it could take four passengers in comfort. One dark, wet winter's night, Mr Platt gave my mother and me a lift home from a concert in the Princess. As we sat in the back in comfort, looking out on the dark rainy night, it felt like floating in a magical glass bubble; we were warm and dry and insulated from the rest of the world.

One thing all the girls loved to do was dress up. We were lucky because one of my mother's relatives was on the stage. She lived in the south of England, and did an act on stage drawing quick sketch-portraits of people. Her work gave her access to many colourful costumes. She often sent unwanted costumes to us, which we kept in a dressing-up box. When we dressed up, our imaginations ran away with us. We would perform plays and pantomimes and it didn't matter that the costumes weren't always right for the part, a costume was a costume! I have a photograph taken by our schoolteacher in the local park, of me in a group of children, dressed in my Aladdin's costume. I was ten years old and playing the part of Oberon, the King of the Fairies in the junior school production of Shakespeare's *A Midsummer Night's Dream*.

May Day processions were often organised with groups of friends. There were many different processions in the area, some of which were a sight to behold. Our particular group chose one girl to walk at the front of the procession dressed as a bride. She carried a small posy of flowers – real ones if we could get hold of them, artificial ones made from crêpe paper if we couldn't – wrapped with a gold paper doily, and my mother lent her precious wedding veil to make the bride look more realistic. The retinue walking behind the bride was dressed in a variety of odd outfits: an Indian prince, a Guardsman in a bright red jacket, a Chinese mandarin, and other girls bringing up the rear staggered along on high heels borrowed from their mothers. One girl wore a red fox fur and another reeled along trying to control a skunk fur about six feet long with tails at each end – both furs were borrowed from my mother.

We wended our way up and down the roads, rattling a tin to collect the money we needed, to buy sweets, cakes and lemonade for our May Day tea party, which we held in the yard at the back of our house. Most people were amused by the sight of our procession; they would smile and give a small donation of a couple of pence towards our feast. Once we'd bought the food, we spread a paper tablecloth over a three-legged stool (made from an old wooden washing dolly), then we sat and ate our feast of meat paste sandwiches, iced fairy cakes, heart-shaped biscuits with coloured icing and bottles of lemonade. Our dolls came to the party, sitting propped up alongside the stool, and we would pretend that they were real people, asking them what they would like to eat and drink. If there was any money left over after we'd bought our food for the party, for a couple of pence we would buy a Chinese novelty in a small packet with

Chinese writing on the outside. Inside the packet was a flat wedge of coloured tissue paper. We would put the tissue paper in a glass tumbler full of water, and as we watched, the paper slowly unfurled to become a beautiful bright-coloured flower which floated gently in the water, its petals wafting as it moved about in the glass – we were fascinated. How did this happen?

When the weather was not good enough to play out, we'd go along to St Mary's Church Walton on the Hill, to the children's corner at the back near the christening font. There were books to read, toys to play with and often someone who would come in to read a story; something from the Bible, one of Aesop's Fables, or one of our own favourite children's stories. The church had a strange musty smell, even on bright sunny days, and the fragrant floral displays for special occasions, such as a wedding, Easter, a christening or a funeral, could not mask the musty odour. The church crypt remained a mystery to us, the door to the entrance was kept locked, and there was a chill in the air as we passed it, but it may just have been a draught from under the door. Was it really full of rows of skeletons as we imagined? It was somewhere we never wanted to go, and something we never wanted to find out.

We could always find something to do to keep ourselves amused. We didn't need expensive toys or lots of money to spend to make us happy and for many children the money was not there to spend. There was a sense of freedom of movement and activity which children have lost nowadays; we could disappear for hours and no one worried, so long as we were back in time for dinner.

Roller skating was very exciting. It was also the only pastime, apart from cycling, which needed expensive equipment. Roller skates with ball bearings in the wheels were the best ones to have. My sister and I had to share a pair, as a result of this we often sped along on one skate each. The sole of one shoe would be worn down, while the toe on the other shoe would be badly scuffed, much to the despair of our mother.

Sometimes we would have a picnic in Walton Hall Park. It was about a quarter of an hour's walk away from our house, and we would take some fruit and sandwiches to eat and a bottle of lemonade to drink. Before we went to the park, we were given strict instructions not to go into the long grass and not to speak to any strange men or take sweets from anyone we didn't know. If strangers approached us, we were to walk away. We were never told why and at our age we didn't understand; we didn't take too much notice, though, as we couldn't wait to be off.

Once in the park, we were free to enjoy ourselves. We picked buttercups and held them under our chins to test whether or not we liked butter; we puffed away at dandelion clocks to guess the time, and sat on the grass making daisy chains, trying to see who could make the longest one before the stalks snapped.

After our picnic, we would wander round to the bandstand in the middle of the park, to see if anything interesting was on. It was a white crescent-shaped Art Deco-style building. Metal chairs with black frames and dark green wooden seats were set out in semi-circular rows so anyone who wanted to could sit and watch a performance or listen to the band play. It was usually a brass band. The bandstand was also used for open-air performances by other bands, small orchestras, groups of tap-dancers, local choirs or the Amateur Dramatic Society. Next to the bandstand was a small tearoom which sold ice creams, water ices, lemonade, biscuits and pots of tea.

There were two lakes in the park. The largest lake was for rowing boats, which could be hired by the hour from a man with a big watch; he was very strict with anyone who was out for more than the hour allowed, even a few minutes over meant an extra hour would have to be paid for. The boathouse had a small clock tower to make sure rowers could keep an eye on the time – there was no excuse for bringing the boat in late.

The smallest lake was more like a shallow pond, where children could catch newts and small fish called sticklebacks. Newts are fascinating little creatures, like small lizards with tiny webbed feet like stars, which tickled as we let them walk over our hands. When we found some frogspawn, we took it home and put it in a jam jar with string tied round the top. We would look after it, carefully feeding the tiny frogs with bits of meat when they emerged from their jelly cocoon. If we were lucky, the frogs would grow big enough for us to release them back into the lake.

On the way home from the park, if we had time, we went round the back of the church and through to the cobbled courtyard which housed the Smithy, where the blacksmith shoed horses for the local tradesmen. We were allowed to watch, peering into the dark, mysterious interior, so long as we stood quietly in the doorway and didn't shout or make any noise which would disturb and frighten the horses that were already nervous at being in the Smithy.

The blacksmith was huge; he towered over us like a giant, and he had a shiny red face which gleamed with perspiration and huge hands to hold the big shire horses' legs on his knees while he hammered the shoes onto their hooves. To protect himself from the dirt and heat he wore a long, thick, black leather apron.

His assistant, who worked the bellows to keep the furnace glowing fiercely, was of a similar size and they worked together as a team.

The furnace belched out flames and sparks flew high up into the air, lighting up the darkness. The noise of the hammers was deafening as they hit the red-hot horse shoes, hammering them into shape on the anvil. Added to all this was the strong pungent smell and puffs of smoke as the hot shoes were nailed onto the horses' hooves. We were both fascinated and frightened at the same time as we gazed into this dark cavernous noisy place. The site of the old Smithy is now occupied by a block of flats and a car park.

One day in the spring of 1939, my friend Pamela came round to show me the new cart which her grandfather had just made for her. It was made to collect the horse manure which he needed for his allotment. He had built it from pieces of wooden orange boxes, collected from the greengrocers, then carefully sanded to remove any splinters. The undercarriage and steering were made from the wheels, spindles and handle of an old pram. A thick piece of rope was attached to the front of the cart to pull it along. With no horse manure in it, the cart was just big enough for Pamela to sit in and be pulled along. With a cart like this to ride on, I was only too keen to help with the manure collection.

Pamela's grandfather had retired from a lifetime working indoors as a bank clerk. In his retirement, the allotment allowed him to spend his time outdoors and to fulfil his long-held wish to grow his own vegetables and roses. Pamela's family lived in the next road, in a turn-of-the-century terraced house similar to ours, with a small front garden and a back yard. Renting an allotment was a good way for men to grow fresh vegetables for their families. It was also a place for them to relax in the evenings and weekends after work. When they tended their plots, the allotments became a social place to meet, have a chat, a quiet smoke and perhaps a glass of beer.

The allotments were about half a mile away, alongside the railway embankment. In those days allotments were very much in demand, and Pamela's grandfather had had his name on the waiting list for some time. Finally, someone had died, so his name had come up. Because many everyday household things were delivered by horse and cart, we would be assured of a steady supply of warm, slightly steaming, golden brown manure to make the vegetables grow and the roses bloom.

Milk, in bottles, was delivered every day on a horse-drawn, covered cart, with a small open-sided cab at the front, which made it easy for Charlie, the milkman, to nip in and out as he stopped at each house. Daisy, the milkman's horse, was a quiet creature with thick beautiful eyelashes and a gentle nature, who loved to be patted by everyone. Daisy never needed to be prodded or shouted at to move on, she watched Charlie carefully out of the corner of her eye, and as soon as he took a bottle off the cart, she moved on a few paces and stopped at the next house.

Coal was delivered on a big open horse-drawn cart. The cart was an impressive sight, with the name and address of the coalman proudly displayed in gold letters painted on a black background along the side; the spokes of the wheels were painted a bright fire-engine red. The coalman sat high on a seat at the front. Coal was stacked in rows behind him in hundred-weight sacks. There was a set of iron scales for weighing out the coal.

Sometimes a customer only wanted half a hundred weight, and a bag had to be split. It took a big strong horse to pull a cart bearing two or three tons of coal.

The coalman's horse was a magnificent beast, a shire horse with masses of white shaggy hair on his fetlocks and a long, flowing mane. He was held in the cart by a black leather harness on his back, attached to the wooden shafts. The coalman dropped his loads of coal down the steel manhole covers into customers' coal cellars. For those who didn't have a coal cellar, he would carry the sack of coal round to the back of the house and put it in their coal shed. The horse snorted and stamped his feet impatiently if he had to wait too long. To protect him from the rough coal bags, which he carried on his back, the coalman wore a sleeveless jacket of thick black leather with metal studs. A few main roads in our area were still cobbled, and when the horse's feet slipped on them, sparks flew from his hooves. One of the dares that we played in our games of Truth-or-Dare was to run under the belly of the coalman's horse. I did it once and was so frightened that I ran off home to recover.

The coalman's horse led the May Day parade in the park. We hardly recognised him; dressed in all his finery he was completely transformed and was now a sight to behold. His huge brown body was brushed, burnished and gleaming in the sunlight. Horse brasses set on black leather straps hung about his neck, and his halter was decorated with the rosettes that he had won over the years for being 'Best of Breed'. On his head he wore a vividly coloured plumed headdress, which rose high in the air and all the small brass bells hanging from it jingled and jangled noisily as he tossed his head.

The horse was a proud and wonderful animal. For the parade his mane had been elaborately knotted and entwined with brightly coloured ribbons and his tail was perfectly plaited. He knew he looked good. As the brass bands played he put on a magnificent show as he snorted, pawed the ground and stomped up and down before the admiring crowd.

The summer of 1939 was warm and golden, and one I remember with pleasure. Though the storm clouds of war were gathering, as seven-year-olds we were not really aware of the seriousness of the situation. There was no television to watch, and what news we heard came via the radio, newspapers and the Pathé newsreels at the cinema. The reporting of news was a serious and intelligent business. We had no way of knowing that this would be the last summer for many years that our lives would be quite so carefree.

On the hottest summer afternoons, when the heat of the sun made the tar in the road blister and bubble, my friend Pamela and I would sit idly on the edge of the pavement, bursting the bubbles in the tar with our fingers, waiting for a horse or a car to go past. As we casually poked at the sticky black tar bubbles, we talked about some of the questions we did not understand. Why was it that when we caught German measles we didn't come out in small Swastikas? (We were quietly disappointed about this.) Where did babies come from? We weren't convinced about the gooseberry bush story – and why did the gooseberries need a good dose of Epsom Salts? This couldn't have anything to do with babies, wasn't it a laxative for grown-ups? Having failed to answer any of these questions, we went home with tar stuck all over our fingers, socks and sandals, much to our mothers' despair. The tar had to be removed by rubbing it with small knobs of butter. We were given stern warnings of 'Do not do that again'.

The rag-and-bone man sometimes trundled by with his thin, bony horse and dilapidated old cart, giving out brightly coloured balloons in return for any old clothes and odds-and-ends of household articles that were no longer needed.

When the little merry-go-round appeared, we rushed home to bring out the jam jars we had collected. The merry-go-round was mounted on a low square cart, pulled by a very patient pony called Jim. The pony was led by the owner of the cart, an old man with a white beard, who we thought looked like Father Christmas' brother. In exchange for the jam jars, we could hop onto the cart and choose to ride on a prancing golden horse, a bright-red fire engine with a bell we could ring by pulling a rope, a blue and white milk float with white wooden bottles, a steam engine with a whistle, a terrifying dragon with red flames spurting from his mouth or a police car with a blue light. While the old man cranked the handle, the merry-go-round rotated slowly to the sound of a barrel organ. My favourite ride was the fire engine because clanging the bell made a terrific noise.

As the summer went by, wonderful things began to appear from the allotment. The rhubarb flourished and produced sticks as thick as my arm. The roses bloomed profusely, almost weighing down the bushes with their huge, heavily scented flowers. In return for my help in collecting the manure, I was given some of the produce from the allotment to take home. My mother cooked the rhubarb with brown sugar and a generous pinch of ginger, to enhance the flavour. As children we didn't always like the strong taste of rhubarb, but it came under the category of 'this will do you good' – there was no argument to be had, so down it went! Nothing was wasted; the rhubarb leaves were boiled in an old pan to produce a thick, khaki-coloured poisonous liquid, which was a wonderful natural insecticide and killed off all the aphids, whitefly and greenfly.

The savoy cabbages and spring greens were enormous and squeaked with freshness when picked. A sprinkle of bicarbonate of soda was added to the water while the cabbage was cooking to help it keep its bright green colour. I remember being trapped by my mother in the corner, between the kitchen sink and the back door, and made to drink the water in which she had boiled the cabbage. This, she promised me, would give me beautiful skin when I grew up. She was right, of course, as all mothers are – I constantly receive compliments on my lack of wrinkles. Why was it, we wondered, that everything that would 'do you good' always tasted so awful?

My father loved roses, but he was unable to do much gardening because of his artificial leg. Once a week in season, from the allotment, I brought home a deep red, velvety rose for him. His favourites were Ena Harkness and Josephine Bruce, both of which were a beautiful ruby red colour and had a heavily scented smell. My father wore his rose with pleasure in his buttonhole every Saturday and Sunday when he went to see his friends for a drink and a chat in the Black Horse Inn. When I had a garden of my own I planted a bush especially for him, so that I would be able to give him his favourites roses.

When I returned home after each manure collection, I was marched to the sink where my hands and arms were mercilessly scrubbed with Lifebuoy Soap. The soap was rusty red in colour and smelled strongly of disinfectant. I had to sit on the back step until my 'aroma' had gone!

When war finally broke out we were enthusiastic members of the 'Dig for Victory' campaign. My mother saved all her potato peelings and tea leaves, which helped to feed the hens at the back of the ARP hut. They provided us with plenty of brown and white eggs. When the eggs were softly boiled, we dipped our Hovis soldiers into their rich golden yolks (though for me it was with some trepidation, as I did not like eggs at all!).

In winter, the dark nights and the bad weather meant we spent very little time outside. After school we went straight home. The one treat that we had during the week was our Tuesday night visit to the Band-of-Hope meeting at the Methodist Mission. We queued up noisily outside the single-storey red brick hall, and once inside, having paid our 2*d*, we began the meeting by singing some rousing hymns. We would then watch lantern slides for about an hour, thrown onto the white wall by an old projector. The projector was made from dark brown highly polished wood with brass fittings, and it had a big lens, like a giant eye. The slides were put into the projector in pairs and were pushed slowly back and forth by hand. The talk was mainly of the missionary work being done in Africa, but we also saw slides of lots of wild animals and beautiful images of the African landscape. To finish off, before we went out into the night, we sang a spirited version of 'Jesus Wants Me for a Sunbeam'. On the way home, with our heads filled with tales of adventures in 'darkest Africa', we managed to scare ourselves silly by growling at each other and pretending to be man-eating wild animals.

Sometimes on a Saturday morning, I went to one of the local cinemas where they held sessions showing cartoons and films made especially for children. They were pretty noisy performances, as the boys and some of the girls took the opportunity to shout at the films because their parents weren't there.

We had large books containing cardboard figures to be cut out, and in the better ones the figures were outlined with perforations and could be simply pressed out. These books contained a selection of outfits to dress the figures and each outfit had small paper tabs on, which were folded round the figures to dress them in stylish day dresses, winter outfits, and for the female figure a wedding dress, and for the male figure a morning suit. These books would keep us busy for hours. Jigsaw puzzles were also very popular; we did ours on pieces of plywood, so an unfinished one could be put aside and kept to finish another day.

There was a large cardboard box in our toy cupboard, called a Compendium of Games. It contained Ludo, Snakes and Ladders, draughts, Dominoes, two dice, a shaker cup for the dice and counters for the games. The games would keep us busy for hours, often with heated arguments over who had – or had not – cheated! When my mother and father had the time they would join in, making the games more exciting and stopping the arguments between my sister and me. My mother used to say, 'I am sure no two other children in the world argue like you two do.' My father showed me how to play draughts, and then later on, when I was a bit older, he taught me to play chess.

The Bagatelle game was mine, given to me one Christmas as a present from Auntie Liz. It was a sloping wooden board about two feet long and shaped like an arched window. Brass nails were hammered into the surface. To play the game, small shiny steel balls were pushed with a wooden stick, and allowed to roll down the slope bumping between the brass nails. Holes set into the slope were numbered, giving your score when the ball went into a hole.

One game we played, which I am thoroughly ashamed of now, was 'knock and run'. We drew lots and one of our group had to go and knock on the door of a chosen house then run away. We hid round the corner to see what happened when the door opened.

By a strange coincidence, the house chosen was nearly always the home of Mrs Thomas, a small, plump Welsh woman who was a widow and lived on her own. She dressed soberly, even in summer, in a black dress and round her neck was a long string of black jet beads. Her greying hair was pulled back severely from her face and wound into a bun. We were convinced she was a witch. This made the game more exciting by adding a touch of danger, because we believed that if she caught us, she would either cast a spell on us or gobble us up. Of course, she never did! When she found out where I lived, she came round to complain to my mother, who promptly gave me a wallop. I was made to write a letter of apology and not allowed to play out for a week.

We played marbles with small glass balls of bright vivid colours. The ones we prized most were called parrots, dense white with either thick red or blue twirly patterns in them. We nicknamed the game 'allys', because the marbles resembled alabaster. It was like a game of bowls in miniature. As a marble was rolled, the next person in line tried to hit it with one of their own. If you hit the marble, you could claim it as your own. We played the game along the pavements or sometimes, if the weather was dry, in the gutter. If you really wanted a marble in a particular colour and someone else had it, a system of 'swaps' was in place. You could offer two or maybe three for the one that you wanted.

The girls loved to play with their dolls and prams. The best dolls had china heads, with eyes which opened and closed and lips which were slightly apart, showing beautiful little white teeth. Their bodies were made from either papier mâché or wood. Some of the cheaper dolls were made entirely from pink celluloid, and were quite dangerous, because they were highly flammable and could, therefore, never be played with near an open fire.

My sister and I had two dolls with china heads. The one which belonged to my sister had golden curls and lovely blue eyes surrounded by long black lashes, which opened and closed when she was laid down. Her rosebud mouth was partly open to show a perfect set of small white teeth. She was so pretty, my sister named her Elizabeth, after Princess Elizabeth. The other doll we had to share. It had no hair, but rumples on its china head to look like hair, and plump rosy cheeks. It was a pleasant but not very pretty doll, so we called it Billy. Because the dolls were the size of real babies, we dressed them in our own old baby clothes.

I had two dolls of my own. One was a small, black china doll, with lots of black curly hair and gold earrings. She was dressed in a red and white check dress, with a white frilly pinafore and was called Jemima. The other doll was quite small and made from composition, rather like papier mâché. Only her head and arms moved, and she was named Emma.

We had two doll's prams, which my sister and I had to share. One had a navy blue body with big wheels and a fabric hood, like a normal baby's pram, and the other was a small folding pram called a Tan-Sad. It was made from beige leatherette and had a little wooden tip-up rest for the doll's feet. I had a doll's cot, which was given to me as a gift from Auntie Liz one Christmas. It was wooden and painted pale blue, with transfers of baby bears on the sides. One side slid up and down on rails and it had four small castors. With its straw-filled mattress and pillow resting on a wooden lattice base, it was just like a real baby's cot. After many years in the loft and some refurbishment, it now belongs to my great-niece.

We played house, dressed and undressed the dolls, then went for walks with our 'babies'. We also had dolls' tea parties. My sister had a tea set for dolls that was kept in a cardboard box, covered with pretty, pink, flower-patterned paper. The set had six small cups and saucers, six tea plates, a milk jug, a sugar basin, and a teapot. It was cream china with a dainty gold and brown pattern; my sister still has a few of the items that have survived to this day. To drink at the party we bought dandelion and burdock cordial from the herbal shop behind the Smithy. Watered down, the dark brown liquid looked just like tea, and we would fill the teapot with it. We ate small chocolate wafers and jelly babies, and when we bought the food for the parties, we didn't eat any of it on the way home. We were not allowed to eat in the street, as it was considered bad manners. We ate at meal times, sitting at the table. The dolls sat around on makeshift stools as our guests.

We didn't worry if one of our best dolls became 'sick', such as their eyes falling into the back of their heads, an arm or a leg coming loose, or their wig coming unstuck, we would take them straight round to the 'Dolls' Hospital'. The man who owned the toyshop also owned the Dolls' Hospital, and he ran his 'surgery' from a room at the back of his toyshop.

To replace the eyes, he would carefully turn back the hair, and insert into the socket a new pair of either wax or glass eyes to match the originals, before he carefully replaced the hair. It was easy to do this, because the heads were hollow and the top of the head was open under the wig. The arms and legs were easily replaced, as they were held onto a central hook inside the body, by strong, twisted elastic bands. Once they were replaced, the doll was as good as new.

The most beautiful doll I had ever seen belonged to my friend Pauline. It was called a Shirley Temple doll, and had been made to look like Shirley Temple, a child film star of the 1930s, who sang and danced her way through many films. Shirley Temple dolls were made in America and were difficult to buy in this country. Pauline was lucky, her cousin, Charlotte, had come over from America for a visit and brought one with her as a present. The doll came in a large box with a cellophane lid, so we could see her without touching her or taking her out of the box. She was dressed in a frilly pink and white organdie dress, white buckskin shoes and short white socks. Brown silky ringlets of hair tumbled down to her shoulders. I remember one night during the war, when Pauline's house was hit by a small incendiary bomb and one of the bedrooms was partially destroyed by fire, my first thought was, 'Oh, I hope that beautiful doll is safe!' When I returned the next day, I was happy to see the doll was still in perfect condition.

My Teddy and I went everywhere together. He sits proudly on my knee in a studio portrait of me taken when I was three years old. He had lovely big glass eyes, a golden synthetic-fur body, which was stuffed with small wood shavings, and he growled when he was tipped backwards and forwards. My mother made a pair of black pants, a white shirt and a red satin bow tie for him; he looked so smart. Many years later, he still had a bit of life left in him, and I gave him to my son to play with for a while.

Sadly, when he was about fifty years old, Teddy began to disintegrate. The cotton backing of his fur had started to turn to powder, his body was splitting open and small dust mites had set up home in his wood shavings. One bright Sunday morning, I took Teddy to the local tip.

Chapter Six

HOLIDAYS

During the long summer holidays, my mother made sure that we went on plenty of day trips to keep us occupied. We were lucky, public transport was reliable then and we lived within easy reach of sandy beaches and many interesting places, including museums, art galleries, seaside towns, places of historical interest and some lovely parks and gardens.

One holiday that I remember well was a group holiday for the women and children of our family. We stayed at a boarding house near Prestatyn in North Wales. The family members who went were my mother, my sister and myself; Auntie Elsie and her three children, Betty, Margaret and Billy; Auntie Margaret and her two children, Dorothy and Alec and Auntie Emma, who was unmarried, but she was always included in whatever we did. We shared six double beds in three huge bedrooms. It was great fun being on holiday as part of such a large family group. The food in the boarding house was good home cooking, with plenty to feed our healthy appetites that we worked up as we spent our days running around in the open air and sunshine.

The boarding house was a rambling Victorian villa, and opposite it was a park with a boating lake to sail model boats on, a field where a white horse and some small ponies grazed and beyond that, the sandy beach. We used to watch the toy yachts and clockwork boats sailing on the lake, then go off to feed the ponies with some carrots and bread. In the afternoons, we went down to the beach, to paddle, build sandcastles and make sand-pies. Late in the afternoon, with our sandals and hair full of sand, we came back to the boarding house, exhausted and happy, with buckets full of shells and bits of things we'd found on the beach. After supper, too tired to talk or even wash properly, we would fall into bed.

The men in the family did not come on this holiday for several reasons. Auntie Elsie's husband was away at sea with the Merchant Navy, usually for months at a time. Auntie Margaret's husband was a workaholic joiner, dedicated to producing the beautiful objects of his trade, very rarely taking time off from his work. My father only had ten days' summer holiday, and so needed a rest, not only from work, but also from his children, choosing to stay at home. Besides, he was never keen to stray too far away from home and often shy about meeting new people.

Our day trips required some preparation, as we always took our own food. Sandwiches were egg and cress, ham, tinned salmon and cucumber, or beef paste. Not all of these on one picnic of course! We also had homemade sausage rolls, fairy cakes, fruit, usually apples or pears, and sometimes a bottle of lemonade or sarsaparilla to complete the feast.

A daytrip to Chester meant we had to set out quite early because it was 'over the water', the water being the River Mersey. The food was prepared and packed in my mother's shopping basket the night before. First, we had to catch a tram down to the Pier Head in Liverpool, then the ferry boat to Birkenhead. The ferry boat was the most exciting part of the trip. We stood at the Pier Head waiting for the boat to dock, and once it had, the side of the deck slid back and a ramp came down. We had to wait behind a barrier until all the passengers got off before we raced aboard, to my mother's shouts of 'Be careful!' From the top deck we'd watch the ships in the river, coming and going from countries all round the world and wonder what it would be like to travel to exotic places with strange-sounding names. Our ferry ride across the Mersey was only a short crossing, and in our excitement we ran around the decks, playing tick and hide-and-seek.

In Birkenhead, the buses were lined up at the depot by the landing stage, waiting for the ferry boats to dock. We caught a green double-decker bus all the way to Chester. As soon as we got on the bus, we ran upstairs to the front seats, where we could have a good view of the countryside. Once in Chester, we went for a walk around the old sandstone walls to look at the monuments and Roman remains. From the walls there were views right over the city. Next, we went to the park to play for a little while before we went down to the river to feed the ducks and watch the boats go by. We sat on benches on the rows of steps alongside the river Dee, overlooking the weir, and ate our picnic lunch. Sometimes, if we had time, we went for a ride on one of the passenger boats which sailed up and down the Dee.

If the weather was not too good, we went for a walk along the Rows, the raised wooden covered walkways which are an unusual feature of Chester and very famous. The two tiers of the Rows were lined with shops, selling such a wide variety of things: toys, sweets, shoes, leather goods, antique furniture, fine silver, beautiful jewellery, many ladies' outfitters and Browns of Chester, a well-known department store. For anyone who wanted to have a sit down and rest their weary feet, there were plenty of tearooms serving afternoon teas.

A visit to Chester Cathedral was always the last thing we did before we caught the bus back to the ferry. Built of red sandstone, Chester Cathedral is a cavernous old place with a musty smell and there was so much to explore there: nooks and crannies, side chapels and hidden stairways. We looked at all the old flags, hanging in one of the chapels, bearing the battle honours of local regiments, some of which were tattered and threadbare. We read the names and dates of the people buried in the tombstones set into the floor and the walls, and if the organ was playing, we listened to the music. Chester Cathedral is an ancient place, founded in 1092, dedicated to St Werburgh, an Anglo-Saxon princess.

The quadrangles enclosed within the walls were quiet havens, with well-kept lawns, rose beds and shrubbery; one of them had a small pond with white water lilies. My mother would sit and have a rest while we wandered round the cloisters and read out loud the names of the saints in the small stained-glass windows set low into the stone walls around the cloisters. As we did so, we tried to imagine what it must have been like to have been a monk here hundreds of years ago, particularly in the winter, with no heating, when the wind would have whistled and howled around the gloomy open spaces, not just in the cloisters but throughout the whole cathedral and their quarters in the abbey.

One of the marvels in the cathedral was a treasure which fascinated me. It was a tiny picture of the *Virgin and Child* painting on a caterpillar's cobweb, set in a small frame on a stand. I stared at the picture, wondering just how the artist had managed to paint the picture without breaking the delicate cobweb. There was also an old grandfather clock in the cathedral, with a card bearing a rhyme by Henry Twells called Time's Paces, which I will always remember:

When as a child I laughed and wept,
Time crept.
When as a youth I waxed more bold,
Time walked.
When as I daily older grew
Time flew.
Soon I shall find, in passing on,
Time gone.
Whence? Why? Whither?

I remembered the rhyme as a child, but it would take many years for me to understand how true it was.

On the way back to catch the bus we called at Quaintway's, the Chester cake shop and restaurant of the Reece's bakery chain. If we'd been good, and even if we hadn't, my mother would say 'Well go on then' and we were treated to an ice cream. One of Reece's Neapolitan ice cream wafer sandwiches, with layers of vanilla, strawberry and chocolate ice cream – a doorstop of an ice cream, so thick I could just about get my small hand round it – was, in my opinion, simply out of this world. It was so big that it would be melting and running down my fingers before I'd finished it.

No matter where we went on our day trips, my mother would try to make sure we would be back home in time for her to cook our evening meal, so it was ready when my father came home from work. On days out when she thought maybe we wouldn't get back in time, she would leave something prepared for him, with a note. Usually we all sat down to eat together at about half past six in the evening, and my father would listen to the news on the radio, to catch up with what was happening in the outside world.

West Kirby was another one of my favourite places. Again, this meant a long journey. We caught a tram to the underground station, where, armed with buckets and spades, we caught a train on the Wirral line, which took us under the Mersey all the way to West Kirby, the end of the line. The sand here was lovely to play in. Across the sand stood three tidal islands, lumps of red sandstone, sitting in the Dee estuary. Hilbre Island was the biggest of the three islands, while Middle Eye and Little Eye were merely tiny uninhabited islets. We followed the tide out and walked to the islands across the wet sand, reaching them at low tide, which gave us the longest time to spend on the islands before the tide turned. We had to keep a watchful eye on the time and the turn of the tide, to make sure we were never caught out and left stranded on the rocks.

We kept our rubber and canvas pumps on to walk about on the sand because, apart from the odd broken lemonade bottle left on the beach, there were also lots of cockle shells, tiny pink shells, long thin razor shells, a few stranded jellyfish rotting in the sunshine and something which I hated to walk on – worm casts – scattered across the sand. We played in the many rock pools left by the outgoing tide. Trapped in them were dozens of small fish, tiny transparent shrimps and little sand-coloured crabs. Darting about in the water there were also some strange wiggly worms and other minute little things, but we never knew what they were.

After each trip to West Kirby we insisted on taking a few of the small crabs home with us in our buckets, with a little seawater and some sand to keep them happy. My mother tried to stop us from doing this, and she reminded us that no matter what we did they would not survive the journey, but we wouldn't listen. Sure enough, she was right; they were always dead before we reached home.

When we were thirsty at the seaside we would drink water from one of the elaborate old drinking fountains. Built in Victorian times, they each had the year of their installation carved into the stone. They were usually built of red brick and stone, with a small metal basin underneath the tap to catch the water. A metal drinking cup was attached to the fountain by a chain. The chain was long enough to reach the tap to fill it up and for us to lift it to our lips. We washed the cup thoroughly first, because it had been used by so many people. There was always a queue at the fountains, not only to drink the water, but people wanted to splash water onto their feet to wash the sand off before putting their sandals on to go home.

Like most seaside places, there was a shop selling coloured beach balls, buckets and spades, beach hats, pumps, hand-held windmills and sticks of rock in a variety of different colours, sizes, shapes and flavours. The shop hired out shiny dark brown earthenware teapots, filled with hot water to make tea, at sixpence a time. A deposit of 1s had to be left to make sure the pot and the tin tray were returned. We took our own tea and sugar in small folded parcels of greaseproof paper, a medicine bottle full of milk and some Bakelite cups. We were able to enjoy a nice cup of tea.

When we tired of the beach, we changed out of our bathing costumes, packed up and walked up the hill to the picnic area around the monument, a war memorial in the form of a bronze statue of a soldier, set high on a rocky sandstone outcrop, surrounded by gorse and heather, gazing out over the Dee estuary towards the Welsh hills. My mother would sit on one of the seats near the statue and read a book or a magazine, while my sister and I played hide-and-seek amongst the heather and very prickly gorse bushes. If we found a sprig of 'lucky' white heather, we would take it home.

Neston, an area a few miles further round the coast on the Wirral Peninsula, was a place which held fond memories for my mother. As a young woman she used to go swimming there with her friends, in an open-air swimming pool. She was a very good swimmer and won many medals, it is difficult to imagine winning anything in the cumbersome swimming costumes which women had to wear in her day.

My mother knitted woollen bathing costumes for me and my sister, in green and yellow wool, with plain green bottoms and stripy tops. The costumes fitted well when they were dry, but as soon as they got wet the weight of the water made them sag right down, making us look like half-drowned bumblebees. I have a photograph of me, a scrawny bag of bones, sitting on the beach wearing my costume. The memory of our woollen costumes still makes me smile. Eventually we had nice new swimming costumes that my mother bought for us at a department store.

❖❖❖

Living where we did, we had easy access to some of the finest museums and art galleries outside of London. They were the Liverpool Museum, the Walker Art Gallery and the Lady Lever Art Gallery. Trips to these places were saved for rainy days.

The famous Egyptology section in the museum was fascinating; it gave a glimpse of things mysterious and exotic. There was a large collection of ancient artefacts, among them large stone pots decorated with figures, some beautiful jewellery which had come from the tombs discovered in the Pyramids by British archaeologists in the 1920s, old broken pieces of pottery and many examples of an ancient mysterious writing called hieroglyphics. The best things of all were the mummies, wrapped in bandages lying in huge stone coffins. They were quite frightening. I was scared that one day one of them would come back to life, strip off its bandages, rise up out of its stone sarcophagus and chase me round the museum. During the war, most of these precious treasures were taken away and stored elsewhere for safe-keeping – rumour had it they were hidden down the salt mines in Cheshire.

The Walker Art Gallery, next door to the museum, was a treasure house full of beautiful paintings by famous artists, including Joseph Turner's *The Fighting Temeraire*. One room contained an impressive collection of classical white marble statues standing on pedestals, which filled the room. Walking round the statues was like walking through a crowd of people. There were lots of busts around the walls set in niches and on small stands. What made it very interesting and exciting was that most of the statues were nude, a source of much amusement for me but a great embarrassment for my mother.

We occasionally visited Liverpool Anglican Cathedral. It was, and remains, in terms of its sheer size, the largest cathedral in Western Europe. The massive red sandstone building stands on the highest point in the city, making it visible for many miles around; it dominates the skyline and can be seen from far away in Cheshire. Designed by the famous architect Sir Giles Gilbert Scott, construction was started in 1903, and in the 1930s, when we were children, it was still not complete.

On one of our visits to the cathedral we went into the old St James' Cemetery in grounds at the rear of the cathedral. Once a quarry, it was converted to a cemetery in 1829. The cemetery is a very unusual place, based on the Cimetière du Père Lachaise in Paris. Closed for burials in 1936, it is the final resting place for up to 60,000 souls. It has three tunnels, a spring reputed to have medicinal properties, and the walls are lined with gravestones.

My mother enjoyed her trips to Southport. Sometimes we went by train and sometimes we went by bus. My mother would stroll down Lord Street, with its Victorian arcades, and enjoy window shopping at her leisure. There were many colourful, beautiful flower displays to see in the gardens along the Promenade behind the Marine Lake, and the famous herbaceous borders and flowerbeds in Rotten Row, alongside Victoria Park, where the flower show is held every August.

Occasionally in Southport we would enjoy the rides in the large permanent fairground, and on our way back to catch the train home, we went to see the model railway and the 'Land of the Little People'. Unfortunately, this attraction has disappeared and is now a supermarket car park.

We never went paddling or swimming in the sea at Southport, because apart from the quicksands, which were very treacherous, the sea was always so far out. The beach near the promenade is wide and sandy and stretches for miles, and was a good place for donkey and pony rides. I have a photograph of my sister and me on a large white pony; I am sitting on the front of the saddle and my sister is clinging onto me as she sits on the back. I look very apprehensive and not too happy, and I am biting my lip. It seemed like such a long way down from there. Often, in an area behind the beach, there were men creating large sculptures of animals, buildings and famous figures in the wet sand, which they painted to make realistic, and they left a hat in the sand to collect money from the admiring passers-by.

Once the war came, our trips to the beaches had to stop for a while, as the barbed wire began to appear. I don't think the Germans were likely to invade this far up on the coast, but the barbed wire was probably put there to make us feel safe.

❖❖❖

During the holidays we were allowed to 'help' my mother with the baking. When we were at school most of the baking was done during the week, and at weekends my mother was often too busy. Not only did this keep us occupied in the holidays, but it was a very good way to teach us the basics of cooking, something which I have never forgotten. My mother didn't have kitchen scales; she measured all the ingredients out by tablespoons, dessertspoons and teaspoons, and sometimes, if she thought the mixture didn't look quite right, she would slip in a bit extra for good measure. Whatever she did, it always turned out perfectly.

I was given a small bowl, some flour, margarine or butter and a spoonful of sugar. I mixed the ingredients carefully by hand, adding some ground ginger, then shaped the mixture into gingerbread men, sticking currants in for their eyes, nose and mouth and down their middles, to represent buttons. By the time I'd played with the dough and the gingerbread men were ready to go into the oven, they were often quite grubby, but I thought they looked pretty good. When they came out of the oven my father would eat some, no matter how good or bad they looked. He would eat them very slowly, while I waited expectantly for his verdict; he would think about it carefully, before pronouncing them 'Very tasty'.

I loved to watch my mother peel a large Bramley apple when she was making an apple pie. She would always try to keep the peel in one piece, and I would watch with bated breath to see if the peel would come off in one long green curl. She put a pinch of cinnamon and a small amount of finely grated lemon peel in her apple pies to give them a lovely flavour, and she decorated the top with pastry leaves, before she finally brushed them with milk and sprinkled sugar over the top. To keep me happy until the pie was ready, I was given a couple of slices of apple to dip into the sugar. The smell of an apple pie baking wafting through the house was so tantalising.

Most Thursdays we would catch a bus to Ormskirk, a small market town a few miles away. Ormskirk held its market every Thursday and Saturday, where farmers and their wives brought their produce into town to sell and there was always such a large selection of vegetables – the potatoes were fresh from the fields with soil still clinging to them (the rich black soil of the South Lancashire plain is ideal for growing potatoes). The market sold huge savoy cabbages, fresh carrots with their fern tops still on, turnips, beetroots, broad beans, French beans and any other seasonal vegetables, such as broccoli, kale and sprouts.

There were two stalls that I remember very well. One was a stall belonging to a small, jolly, Jewish cloth merchant, who came from Manchester and sold a collection of fine tailoring cloths, woollen

worsteds, tweeds and flannel, all cuts of the very best quality. He
was a very good advertisement for his materials, as he wore an
immaculate light grey suit in Prince of Wales check. He didn't have
a tape measure, he measured the cloth by holding it up between
his nose and the fingers of his outstretched arm. A yard was from
the end of his fingers to the tip of his nose. If you only wanted half
a yard, he measured out the yard, folded it over then cut off the
half. My mother always measured the material when she got it
home and it was, she pronounced, 'As near as dammit.'

This simple but accurate measuring system was in complete
contrast to what happened when my mother went into a
haberdasher's shop in Liverpool. Once the material had
been chosen it was carefully laid out flat on the counter, and
then the folded edge was placed in the measuring machine,
which was screwed onto the counter. It was a metal box on
a stand, which had a slit to take the material and a dial on
the top facing upwards, so that the assistant could read the
measurement which had been ordered. As the material was
gently guided through the slit, a needle on the dial went
round. When it reached the length the customer required,
the assistant pressed a lever at the side and a cut was made
at the precise point where the scissors had to start cutting.
No money changed hands at the counters. In the shop, all the
counters were connected via a system of overhead wires and
pulleys to a glass-fronted wooden booth in the corner, where a
cashier sat. I don't remember anyone paying by cheque as very
few people had bank accounts. The cash, plus the bill, was
put in a metal cylinder connected to the wire. The assistant
pulled sharply on the handle at the side, and – hey presto! –
the cylinder shot across the wire to the booth in the corner

where the waiting cashier would take out the cash, keep the carbon copy of the bill and give any change. The system then operated in reverse to return the cylinder to the counter, with any change and the top copy of the bill. A simple mechanical device, but very effective. This system was in operation in many stores, not only the haberdashery.

Another stall in Ormskirk market was owned and run by the man who sold bone china 'seconds'. The china was all made by well-known names such as Wedgwood and Royal Doulton, but each one had a small imperfection and could not be sold as perfect. He juggled with the cups and saucers, spread some plates along his arm, then with a jerk of his elbow brought all the plates into a pile on his large bony hand. He performed amazing feats of dexterity with his china, which kept the crowd entertained. All the time he kept talking with his salesman's patter – 'Come on ladies' – as he encouraged people to buy his 'bargains galore'. Every time I saw him perform, I would wait hopefully for the smash when he dropped something, but he never did. Once, when my mother had bought some china from him, with a wink, he presented me with a pale green china duck, which I kept for quite a long time.

◆❖❖◆

I was growing up, and I suddenly began to realise that in summer when the sun came out my freckles grew browner and much more noticeable. They'd never bothered me until other children, mainly boys, took great delight in calling me names such as 'tea leaves' or 'frecks'. The best things I could think of in response to anyone who shouted these remarks at me was 'skinny banana legs', whether they were fat or thin, and 'sticks and stones may break my bones, but names will never hurt me'. It reached such a point that every time I looked in the mirror, all I could see were the brown freckles covering my face. I complained loud and often to my mother about them and she told me gently that there was nothing I could do, they were sun kisses and I should consider myself blessed.

I was not satisfied by this; surely, I thought, something would work to cure the freckles. First of all I tried cucumber, lying on the bed for hours with slices all over my face. Next, I tried Lacto-Calamine, a pale pink, very powdery lotion which was used to prevent sunburn and to help ease the pain from sunburn already sustained. I spread it thickly over my face where it set into a pale pink face mask, it didn't get rid of the freckles but I went round looking like the bride of Frankenstein, which was worse than the freckles. My final attempt was to try Quasha Chips; a clear lotion which someone told me was good for getting rid of freckles. It had no effect on the freckles, and I later found out it was one of the remedies for killing nits. I think they'd been pulling my leg.

My mother told me off. She said the way I was going on I wouldn't have any skin left on my face by the time I grew up. In fact, I've grown very fond of my freckles, they are part of me and I couldn't imagine myself without them.

I got my colouring from my maternal grandfather. He had sandy red hair, blue eyes, freckles and a fierce temper, and my grandmother had light brown hair and hazel eyes. Of their nine children, two of the boys and two of the girls each inherited sandy red hair, blue eyes and freckles, while the others had brown hair and hazel eyes. Although my mother was one of the brown-haired girls, the sandy red hair and freckles gene skipped a generation and re-surfaced in me and my sister. The sandy hair and freckles gene is a cheeky one that pops up unexpectedly here and there.

Chapter Seven

PARTIES AND PRESENTS

I was a winter baby, born late at night on Saturday, 27th February 1932 – almost a leap-year baby. I often wished I'd been born on 29th February, because it seemed a rare and unusual thing. In the years between a leap year you could decide to have your birthday either the day before, on 28th February or the day after, 1st March.

February, which we knew as fill-dyke month, was always wet and cold. Often, at the end of the month, winter made a last effort and produced a flurry of cold, snowy, slushy weather, so my birthday was always on a dark wintry day. After I started school, I was allowed to have a few friends round for a small birthday tea, on the Saturday nearest to my birthday. The fire was lit in the front sitting room, so that after we'd eaten we could play some games. It was lit early in the day to warm the room up, as the front room was only used for special occasions. The piano stood in the front room, and even when we were doing our piano practice in the winter we had to play with cold fingers.

On my birthday, in spite of the cold, I insisted on wearing a party dress. One of the dresses my mother made for me was in white organdie, embroidered with tiny pink and blue flowers.

I loved it and refused to spoil the look of the dress by wearing a woolly cardigan over it, so I shivered bravely throughout the day. I was told, 'You will catch your death', but I didn't care. I'd waited weeks to wear my new party dress and nothing was going to stop me enjoying my birthday.

One year, I was given a party dress sent to me by my mother's cousin who lived near Ascot, in the south of England. I was so excited, it was the most beautiful dress I'd ever had. Made from peach taffeta, the skirt was a tier of frills set on a net underskirt, and a narrow, pale-green satin sash was wrapped around the dress at the waist. The yoke was edged with a frill and embroidered with tiny seed pearls and minute roses fashioned from very narrow, coloured silk ribbons. When I grew too big for the dress, I cut off the small silk roses and pearls to keep in my memory box.

My birthday cake was a Victoria sponge made by my mother and decorated with white water icing, and it had the right number of pink, yellow and blue candles set in small plastic roses round the edge of the cake and the words 'Happy Birthday Doris' piped in pink in the middle. The food for my birthday tea was mainly ham, meat paste, or salmon sandwiches, small sausage rolls, jelly and blancmange, fairy cakes, chocolate biscuits, a few special cream cakes from Sayers cake shop and tinned fruit with evaporated milk. Sometimes we had ice cream, but it wasn't easy to buy it in the winter and a fridge was a rare thing then.

After we'd eaten we all went into the sitting room to play our games: Pinning the Tail on The Donkey, I Spy, Simon Says, Pass the Parcel and Musical Chairs. For Musical Chairs, my father opened the doors of a large mahogany cabinet to reveal a gramophone turntable and a loudspeaker. He put a record on the turntable then slowly wound up the gramophone. The gramophone was made by a firm called His Master's Voice and had a label bearing a white dog sitting in front of a loudspeaker. My father stopped the music by lifting the arm away from the record, the signal for us to make a very un-ladylike dash for the chairs.

Most of the children at my parties were girls. Only two boys came, and they were only invited because they were the sons of my mother's friends – as far as I was concerned they were not particularly welcome, but I didn't have any choice. At that time in my life I thought boys were noisy pests. It wasn't until I was eleven and in the top class in the juniors that I went to a party where boys were invited and discovered the excitement of playing Postman's Knock!

My friend Marjorie had an auntie who taught domestic science. Her auntie was unmarried and lived with Marjorie and her parents. Marjorie was the apple of her eye and the food she made for her birthday parties was absolutely scrumptious. Jellies were made in classic-shaped glass jelly moulds, but the blancmanges were made in special aluminium moulds in the shape of animals.

A rabbit mould was so versatile. One year, the mould was filled with white blancmange to make a white rabbit, with liquorice sweets for its eyes. The white rabbit was tipped out onto green jelly, which had been chopped up to look like a patch of grass. Small coloured sweets, usually Dolly Mixtures, were scattered on the green jelly to look like flowers in a field.

Another year, the same rabbit mould was filled with chocolate blancmange, on the plate it was decorated with two red glace cherries for eyes and blanched almonds stuck all over its body, to look like spines. It looked just like a hedgehog, sitting on a field of chopped green jelly.

I realised it was important to keep quite friendly with Marjorie, particularly when the time for her birthday was approaching. I couldn't wait to see what her birthday cake would be like and what animal the blancmange would be. One birthday cake was a hollowed-out sponge, filled with small marzipan fruits, and the outside was covered in criss-cross strips of marzipan to make it look like a basket of fruit. Considering the amount of food I ate, it was surprising I remained so skinny.

◄❖:❖►

The night of 31st October was known as 'Duck-Apple Night' (not Halloween, as it is now called). We made a turnip lantern by scraping out the centre of a turnip, cutting round holes for the eyes, a triangular hole for the nose and a slit for the mouth. A piece of string threaded through holes cut in the side of the turnip made a handle, and a night light was lit inside.

It was called Duck-Apple Night because of the games we played with apples. A washing-up bowl was filled with water and placed on the kitchen table, with at least half a dozen small apples floating in it. The object of the game was to keep our hands behind our backs and try to lift an apple out of the bowl with our teeth. We had to wear a waterproof pinny because it was very difficult to pick up an apple as it bobbed about in the water. We ended up with a dripping wet face and more water on the table than in the bowl. Friends came round to our house for the game and we in turn went off to play Duck-Apple at theirs. Even our parents joined in the fun.

Another game we played was trying to bite into small apples that were suspended by their stalks from a strong piece of string stretched between the backs of two dining room chairs, once again while keeping our hands behind our backs. This game was slightly easier because we could bend under the apples to get a tooth-hold and we stayed dry!

While we played Duck-Apple, some shiny, golden brown chestnuts were left roasting on a trivet or in the ash pan of an open fire. When the chestnuts were ready to eat they cracked open with a popping sound. Inside they were a light creamy colour, fluffy and extremely hot; so hot that we had to hold them with a paper napkin, to make sure we didn't burn our fingers. We had homemade ginger beer to drink with our chestnuts, which had been fermenting in a mixing bowl in the kitchen for several days and warmed us on the cold autumn evening.

The other parties that I remember were those on New Year's Eve, held in my Auntie Elsie's house. As the eldest female member of the family, she insisted on everyone going to her house, and it fast became a family tradition. The three sisters who lived together, Elsie, Emma and Lizzie (Auntie Liz to us children, Lizzie to her sisters), worked for hours to produce a buffet, which beautifully presented was set out on Grandma's best white damask tablecloth.

The New Year's Eve party was not really for children, it was for the aunts, uncles, friends and neighbours, who would talk about the old days, making toasts to absent friends, giving news of those who had died during the past year, who had married, had new babies and any other gossip they could possibly think of. Hatches, matches and despatches!

What I looked forward to was the food. After a welcoming drink, we went to the table to help ourselves to the buffet. The large dining room table, with both leaves fully extended, was set with a feast. It seemed to groan under the weight of a variety of cold meats, sausages, pork pies, homemade pickles of every kind, hot jacket potatoes, large bun-loaves, mince pies, what was left of the Christmas cake, and my favourite, a huge trifle liberally laced with sherry and topped with whipped cream.

Alcoholic drinks for the grown-ups were normally kept in the lead-lined compartment of the big old oak sideboard in the dining room, and they were brought out and spread on the top of the sideboard, turning it into a mini-bar. There were bottles of beer, Guinness, sherry, port, gin, whisky, rum and Advocaat. Soft drinks for the children were Dandelion and Burdock, lemonade and homemade ginger beer.

A few minutes before midnight, a dark-haired man would be chosen to play the part of the 'first-footer'. The first-footer was sent outside with a piece of coal, then as soon as twelve o'clock struck he would knock at the door to be let back in, carrying the piece of coal over the threshold to usher in good luck and ensure that there would always be a fire in the hearth. The New Year was greeted with the sound of church bells ringing, people cheering and singing in the streets and the distant thunder of the ships' fog horns on the River Mersey.

Once this ritual was completed, New Year was celebrated with kisses and hugs, then we joined hands for the noisy singing of 'Auld Lang Syne'. Mince pies were handed round and a final toast was drunk to wish everyone good health and a long life. 'Good health and a long life', I thought, was that the best they could wish for? When I was young I could never understand this,

I looked at them in sheer amazement, why didn't they wish for something far more exciting, like chocolates, toys, a new bicycle, money, or longer school holidays? Now I am in my eighties, I can understand why!

There was one final thing to do to end the party. Because the trams and buses stopped running at midnight, we faced a stiff three-mile walk home. As we stood on the steps ready to leave Auntie Elsie's house, everyone, including the children, was given a farewell glass of Advocaat, as it contained brandy, to warm us up for the walk home. I absolutely hated it! Advocaat is a Dutch drink, made from brandy and eggs; it was a sickly, opaque yellow colour with a 'gloopy' consistency. I've never liked eggs in any form and I tried to avoid drinking it, but there was no excuse, down this sickly yellow liquid had to go. Yuk!

The most exciting outing we had during the run-up to Christmas was to go to the grottos. Two department stores had truly magical grottos, one was Lewis's on the corner of Ranelagh Street and Renshaw Street, and the other was Blackler's on the corner of Elliot Street and Great Charlotte Street. Each year, we went to both, but we liked Blackler's grotto the best. The first thing to see when you walked into the shop was a giant Father Christmas and his sleigh, pulled by reindeer, sitting on a silver crescent moon suspended from the ceiling in the high open space in the centre of the store.

The grotto was in the basement, which had been darkened and turned into a series of dimly lit 'caves' full of fairies, gnomes, and a tableau of the stable in Bethlehem. We worked our way through the grotto, looking at the scenes until we reached Father Christmas sitting near the exit. We sat on his knee and told him what we wanted for Christmas. He 'ho-ho'ed' and smiled through his long, white, silky false beard. On our way out of the grotto, one of his gnomes gave each child a balloon, then fairies dipped into one of two bins labelled 'Girls' and 'Boys' and gave each of us a gift-wrapped Christmas parcel. During the rest of the year, Blackler's basement was a treasure trove of pencils, pens, fancy rubbers, coloured paper, crayons, paint boxes, cake decorations for every occasion, candles, toys, and prams and cots.

One Christmas, when I was nearly seven, we had just been to visit Blacker's grotto when on the way out, in the crowd, I got separated from my mother and sister. I wandered round for a while, looking for them, getting increasingly worried. I went up to the ground floor and I still couldn't see them anywhere – there were so many people in the shop and I was not very tall. I thought to myself 'Maybe, they've gone outside to look for me', and so I went out into the street, but they weren't there. I stood on the pavement looking round, wondering what to do next. Perhaps they had gone home and forgotten about me? By now, it was five o'clock and quite dark. Surrounded by strangers, I began to feel a bit panicked, but I didn't cry. Then I thought, 'I don't know where my mother has gone, but I know where my father works and how to get there'. So, keeping tight hold of my balloon in my right hand and holding my Christmas parcel firmly tucked under my left arm, I set off.

It was not an easy journey because I had to cross two main roads then walk up the road at the side entrance to the Mersey Tunnel before coming out onto Dale Street. This was one of the busiest parts of the city and the rush hour was beginning. The Municipal Offices where my father worked were just on the left. I went up the steps and pushed open the big, heavy wooden doors into the lobby. When I walked into his office on the ground floor, my father was very surprised to see me. He looked at me, then looked around and asked 'Where's your mother?' When I told him what had happened, he rang Blackler's right away and told them to tell her where I was, I was quite safe and he would be taking me home. It was nearly half past five and time for him to finish work, so we set off together and walked to the stop to catch the number 22 tram home.

Unfortunately, my mother missed the message that my father had sent to Blackler's; she was already outside searching for me, having left my sister in the care of an assistant in the shop. She decided to come to my father for help. She came running towards my father's office. Crossing Dale Street, she saw me with a man, we appeared to be heading towards a tram with 'Bowring Park' on the front. In the dark, and her panic and confusion, she hadn't recognised my father and she thought I was being kidnapped! She called out to a policeman:

'Stop that man! He's taking my child away!'

The policeman grabbed hold of my father and stopped us both. My mother coming towards us suddenly recognised my father and said, 'Oh, I'm so sorry officer, it's all right, he's my husband', and the policeman let us go.

'You wait till you get home,' she said, turning to me, as it suddenly became my fault. I went home with my father, while my mother went back to Blacker's to collect my sister.

I was in so much trouble; the telling-off went on for days. It seemed so unfair to be told off to this extent, I thought I'd done the sensible thing in the situation. My mother was frantic at the thought of the tram heading for Bowring Park: there had recently been a story in the local newspaper about a child who'd been abducted and found in a 'state' in Bowring Park. At the time I didn't understand what the fuss was about.

At Christmas we were given one 'big' present and a selection of small presents each. When we went to bed on Christmas Eve, before we went to sleep, my sister and I put our bolster cases out for Father Christmas and left them at the bottom of our beds. When we woke up very early on Christmas morning, we dived into the bolster cases. First we would find our big present, such as a doll in a box, a model shop, or a new dressing gown and slippers. The bolster cases were long and narrow, so it took us some time to wriggle down to discover the smaller surprises at the bottom. As we rummaged further down into the cases we'd find the book which we had chosen, a small packet of dates, a tangerine, a beautifully polished shiny red apple, sweets in tiny packages, a net bag of chocolate coins wrapped in gold foil paper and some newly minted bright, shiny, copper coins, carefully saved by my mother in the weeks before Christmas. New copper coins always appeared in December, just in time for Christmas.

If the big present, such as a bicycle, a doll's pram, a doll's cot, a blackboard and some chalk, or a pair of roller skates, was too big to fit in the bolster case, it would be left at the side of the bed. I remember one year I received the game of Ludo and Snakes and Ladders. It was a thick square card which folded over, and on one side it was marked out for Ludo and the other side was vividly decorated with snakes and ladders on a background of tropical trees and plants. Coloured discs and a shaker were also included.

Every Christmas, Auntie Liz, gave me four half-crowns in an envelope. The coins felt so heavy in my hands, and they added up to ten whole shillings! I used to spend some time wondering what to buy with all this money. One of the half-crowns I would put in my money box, to spend later in the year, during my summer holidays.

When I was nearly eight, one of my Christmas presents was a set of three model shops set inside a long cardboard box. The front of the box folded down to reveal the three shops, and when it was open and laid flat it looked like a chequered market-hall floor. Over the top of each shop was a sign, stating the trade: the left-hand shop in the row was a butcher's called 'Mr Lamb', in the middle was a baker's, 'Mr Bun', and on the right a greengrocer's, 'Mr Green'. A counter at the front of each shop had a small model figure next to it, wearing the appropriate outfit for his shop. The figures were freestanding and could be moved around.

Mr Lamb, the butcher, wore a straw boater hat and an apron with wide blue and white stripes. His shop had a metal rail with small hooks to hang up the tiny legs of ham, loins of lamb, sides of beef and strings of sausages.

Mr Bun, the baker, was plump and he wore a white overall and a tall white hat. On his counter was a selection of bread, cottage loaves, Vienna cobs, a tin loaf, some barm cakes, small currant buns and some fairy cakes.

Mr Green, the greengrocer, wore a green overall, and his counter held a colourful pile of vegetables, a basket of tiny potatoes and a selection of fruit.

The items in the shops were made from a type of composition that looked like icing, was carefully painted, very hard and seemingly indestructible. A small set of scales came with the shops, to weigh out the goods on display.

One Christmas I was given a book that I particularly remember called *Nibs in Clover*. It was the story of a beautiful racehorse that had fallen on hard times; he was stolen, then sold to a man who used him to pull a heavy cart, he was beaten and not given enough to eat, or a decent place to live. When his owner finally found him and rescued him, he was in a sorry state, very thin and almost unrecognisable. He was taken back to the lush pastures of his home ground and spent the rest of his years galloping and rolling freely in a field of plentiful green grass and clover. I spent all Christmas lying on the settee reading the book breaking my heart crying, despite the happy ending. My mother vowed never to let me choose my Christmas book again, as I'd ruined everyone's Christmas with my sobs. In future, I would have to be content with a Girls' Crystal Annual or an adventure story.

If we'd asked Father Christmas for two large presents, we would only have one in our bolster, but the other one would appear on our next birthday with some sweets and presents from other members of the family.

Gradually, over the year, I managed to save some of my pocket money to buy a Christmas present for my mother and father. For my father, it was usually an ounce of some of his favourite Ogden's tobacco and a large box of Swan Vesta matches, or some pipe cleaners and a bundle of multi-coloured wooden spills.

For my mother, I bought some scent from Woolworths, either Californian Poppy or Evening in Paris. The Californian Poppy was in a clear glass bottle with a bright red stopper, the yellow label had a picture of a posy of red poppies. The perfume itself was yellow. Evening in Paris, the perfume by Bourjois, was in a stylish, deep purple almost black bottle with a small silver top. The label, a lighter shade of purple, had a picture of the Eiffel

Tower in silver, with silver stars and a crescent moon in the background. The perfume was pale lavender in colour. I can't really remember what either of them smelt like. My mother loved the presents. She always gave me a big smile, a 'Thank you', and a huge hug and a kiss. Many years later, when I was clearing out my mother's house, in her dressing table drawer I found a small bag containing the bottles of perfume, all unopened.

For my mother's birthday, I bought her two white, fine cotton lawn, lace trimmed, hand-embroidered handkerchiefs, carefully folded and presented in a pretty cardboard box. After she died, I also found many of these, carefully kept in her handkerchief sachet with a small lavender bag, to keep then smelling sweet. I also found all the postcards which my sister and I had sent to her over the years, whenever we went away on holiday, even after we were married. Finding all these treasures kept with love and tucked away for such a long time, reduced me to floods of tears.

My Uncle Bill, the sailor and Auntie Elsie's husband, was a very kind, jolly and generous man, with a booming infectious laugh. He loved to have people around him and throw parties. If he was home in time for Christmas they kept open house. He gave everyone presents, mostly brought from abroad, which made them much more exciting. One Christmas, Uncle Bill booked a box at the theatre for all the family and we went to see the pantomime *Aladdin*. It felt so grand sitting in the box, just like royalty, and I was tempted to wave. When he retired after serving twenty-eight years in the Merchant Navy as a Chief Petty Officer, having survived the nightmares of both the Atlantic and the Baltic convoys, he became very ill with what he thought was an ulcer. He'd had trouble for some time whilst he was onboard ship, but he'd decided to wait until he left the navy to have the 'ulcer' treated. Sadly, the problem was diagnosed as stomach cancer in an advanced stage. The 'shore leave', which he had looked forward to for such a long, long time, was very short indeed. We all missed him very much, and Auntie Elsie was left broken hearted.

Chapter Eight

MY MOTHER

My mother Alice was one of nine children, four boys and five girls. The boys were: George, Samuel, William and Harold, and the girls were: Elsie, Elizabeth, Alice, Emma and Margaret. Her mother had, in fact, given birth to thirteen children, four of whom did not survive. One of the four who died was little Billy, who met with a tragic accident when he was two years old. My grandmother had two ladies who came in to help with the household chores. One Monday, the two ladies were carrying a large wicker basket filled with laundry down the cellar steps, ready to do the washing. They each had hold of one of the handles either side of the basket and Billy was sitting on top of the washing. Billy toppled off the basket and fell head-first down the cellar steps, and died.

My mother, the middle one of the five girls, was a calm gentle person; I don't ever remember her really losing her temper. She had soft hazel eyes and thick, light brown hair and, although as she grew old her hair had gone 'pepper and salt grey', it was still thick and wavy. She put this down to the pure bay rum which one of her brothers, William, a merchant seaman, used to bring home from the West Indies. All the girls rubbed it into their hair to give it a rich gloss. When she was eighteen, my mother was allowed to have her hair cut into a short fashionable style. To look at the photographs before and after, from age fifteen to age twenty, we have gone from the Edwardian era to the roaring twenties.

My mother often told my sister and me stories of her parents and her childhood growing up in a large family and the things they did to amuse themselves. Harry, one of my mother's brothers, was always ready to entertain his brothers and sisters. He had various ways of doing this. They would go down to the cellar, where he showed them how to make blocks of coconut ice, by mixing icing sugar and shredded coconut with a little water. Half the mixture was white and the other half had a few drops of cochineal added to make it a bright pink colour. The mixture was formed into thin strips, then put next to each other, one pink, one white, one pink, one white, until the mixture was formed into a large square. It was then pressed gently together and left to set overnight. Next day it was cut into small squares with each square having some pink and white in it. It was very sweet and crunchy.

Another of his entertainments was his 'donkey' engine. He'd screwed a small engine to a wooden board and connected the output of the engine to a wheel via a thin metal belt. When methylated spirit was put into the engine and lit, the pressure in the engine from the steam made the wheel whizz round and the whistle blow.

The most exciting thing Harry had was a small crystal radio. He tuned it in by tickling the crystal with a thin piece of wire called a 'cat's whisker'. Finding the right station was a tricky operation. Everyone had to sit perfectly still and quiet until he hit the right spot on the crystal.

In 1916, during the First World War, Harry was conscripted into a cavalry regiment, even though he had never ridden a horse! He was fortunate; he came home from the war with just a painful back caused by too much riding over rough territory.

The next to eldest brother, William, was in the Royal Navy. My grandmother dreaded them coming home on leave at the same time – they had fierce arguments about which one of the services was the best to be in, and which one was the bravest. William used to shout there are no back doors in the Navy, you can't run away!

Grandma and Grandpa rarely went away on holiday, the family was too large and it would have been very expensive. The main outings for their family were going on picnics. Grandpa hired a wagonette, a wooden four-wheeled, open, horse-drawn vehicle with wooden slatted seats down the sides and one across the front. Food, cups, saucers, table cloths and plates were taken on the picnic, which took most of the day before to prepare. The picnics were held as far away as Chester. Once the food had been eaten, Grandpa had a snooze and the boys fished and played ball, leaving the girls to do the clearing up. Once that was done, they went off for a walk with Grandma.

The size of the family meant that all of the children had to help with the household chores, and they each had certain jobs to do. Early on Monday mornings, the fire under the copper boiler in the cellar was lit before the two ladies came in to help with the washing. The boys carried the coal up from the cellar to fill the coal scuttles, cleaned all the shoes, swilled the yards at the back of the house and, in fine weather, lifted the carpets outside, where they were hung on the clothes line and beaten with large wicker carpet beaters. Everyday cleaning of the carpets and rugs was done with a stiff broom or a hand-pushed carpet sweeper.

The girls did all the ironing and dusting and cleaned the wooden slats of the Venetian blinds with specially shaped brushes, which looked like the hind legs of poodles. They polished the brasses and helped with the cooking. The kitchen was Grandma's territory, with such a large family to feed, each meal took a long time to prepare.

Meat was plentiful and readily available. My grandfather had a butcher's shop, so he supplied the meat ordered by my grandmother. Fish bought from Charles' fish shop was either a large fresh cod, haddock, or hake, filleted, steamed and served whole on a long fish platter. When my mother married she was already competent at running a house.

Life went by at an orderly pace. The first thing my mother did every weekday morning, as soon as my father had gone to work and my sister and I had gone to school, was to clean and polish the brass door knocker, letter box, door knob and keyhole. She then scrubbed and rubbed the front step with a piece of stone – it was a matter of pride to have the front of the house looking well cared for.

My mother's life was centred round the numerous shopping and household tasks and was, to an extent, controlled by the opening hours of the local shops. Each district had a particular day for half-day closing, ours was Wednesday.

We didn't have fridges, and the only places which had cold storage were the Co-op Dairy and the local butcher. The butcher had a white, wooden, walk-in cold store in his shop. He had his ice delivered, and it was taken off a lorry by men who leant into the back of the lorry, grabbed large square chunks of the ice with big metal claws, then flung it over their shoulders to carry it quickly into the shop.

Mondays were wash days, whatever the weather. Rain, hail, snow or sunshine, the washing had to be done. First thing Monday morning the fire was lit under the boiler in the corner of the kitchen, to heat enough hot water for the washing. While the water was heating, the washing was carefully sorted into piles – whites only, coloureds, and hand-washing, such as socks and woollens.

The whites were washed and boiled first with either Rinso or Oxydol soap powder. Rinso came in a green and yellow box and Oxydol came in a bright orange box covered in dark blue swirls. For the final rinse in clean cold water a little cotton bag containing Dolly Blue dye was dipped into the water, this had the effect of making the whites look whiter. The quality of your washing was judged by the whiteness of your whites as they danced about on the clothes line. Once the whites were out of the boiler, the fire was allowed to go out and the remaining hot water was used for the rest of the washing.

Before putting my father's white shirts into the boiler my mother scrubbed the big double cuffs with a large block of green Fairy Household Soap. The loose collars attached to the shirts by collar studs were put in a round cardboard box and taken to the Chinese laundry for washing and starching, returning as stiff as boards. We took one set in and collected the set from the previous week, which was always ready. The people in the Chinese laundry were so pleasant, they greeted everyone with beaming smiles, no matter how hot or steamy it was in the shop. They were very hard-working and efficient, and the collars and laundry were always ready on time.

On my way to the Chinese laundry to take the collars in, I had to pass a single-storey building called the Billiard Hall. It looked quite dark and mysterious inside and was dimly lit by lights with large green shades. The windows were too high off the ground for me to be able to see what went on inside. Once, when I asked my mother what it was and what the men did in there, with a slight sniff, she said it was a 'Den of iniquity'!

Delicate items, such as silk blouses, underwear, jumpers and woollen socks were washed gently by hand, with Lux Soap Flakes. I loved to run my fingers through these soft, silky, transparent, fine slivers of soap. Net and lace curtains had to be given a final rinse of cream dye to keep their colour.

When my mother was first married, she had a large mangle with wrought-iron sides and big wooden rollers. By the late 1930s, she had a new 'Acme', a small white enamel wringer with white rubber rollers. The top folded down and the handle folded in for easy storage.

Once the washing was dry, the sheets and tablecloths were folded carefully to make sure they did not need much ironing. My sister or I helped my mother with the folding procedure: the sheet was folded in half, then my mother took one end by both corners and I took the other end in the same way, we pulled diagonally across the corners to make sure the sheet was stretched, then we walked towards each other, folded the sheet in half and repeated the pulling and folding three times. The sheet was then put through the wringer.

The ironing was done on Monday evenings after we'd eaten our evening meal. My mother had three irons, made from heavy cast iron – two large ones and one small one. They had to be heated on the gas ring of the cooker. As each iron cooled down during the ironing, it was replaced with one that had just been heated. Ironing was quite a dangerous operation, as the irons were very heavy and very hot. The handle had to be held by a thick, padded iron-holder.

There was a lovely pleasant smell as the hot iron went over the washing which had been dried outside on the clothes line in the fresh air. Sometimes my mother ran the irons quickly over a large block of household soap, to make sure they ironed smoothly. My sister and I were not allowed to do any ironing until we were big enough to hold the irons properly.

If the clothes had become too dry, they were sprinkled liberally with water. We put our fingers into a bowl of water, then flicked them over the clothes and rolled them up for a few minutes to let the water seep in. Pillow cases, linen tablecloths, napkins and the cuffs of my father's shirts were starched; they had to be damp to give them a good smooth finish. Starching not only kept the clothes crisp, but it helped to stop them creasing and made the stains easier to remove.

When the weather was too wet to hang the clothes outside on the line, they were put on the clothes rack in the kitchen. Most families had one, and ours was made from five long wooden slats about eight feet long by two inches wide. The slats were held in place with a curved wrought-iron holder at each end. A rope attached to the rack was threaded through two pulleys in the ceiling, making it easy to pull the rack up and down. The rack was also used for airing the clothes after they had been ironed.

My mother told us something she remembered from her childhood. One day, my grandmother had been ironing all my grandfather's butcher's aprons, ready for the coming week. He had a fresh one each day. They were all sitting nicely on the rack in the kitchen when my grandfather came home. It was a Saturday night and he had been to his monthly Masonic Lodge dinner, where he had eaten and drunk very well. He had a quick temper and as he walked through the kitchen the tapes hanging down from the aprons tickled him on the head. He took a pair of scissors and cut all the tapes off, then without a word he put them on the kitchen table and walked away. My mother looked on in amazement as my grandmother never said a word, but quietly picked up the tapes and went for her sewing basket. The next day my grandfather came home with a bunch of flowers.

The irons were very useful when my mother made brawn, potted beef, or pressed tongue. She had a large iron pan lined with white enamel especially for this purpose. The pan was so heavy I could barely lift it, even with both hands. Once the meat was cooked, it was left in the pan to cool. When it was cool, my mother put a plate on top of the meat, pressed down by the smallest of the irons. The plate was left on until the meat had set in its own juices. The next day the pan was carefully turned over and a perfect mould of meat plopped out, smooth and gleaming. I didn't mind the potted beef, but I refused to eat the brawn and the tongue. I'd seen too much of the bits in the pig's head and the ox tongue before they were cooked.

Because Monday was such a busy day for my mother, our evening meal was made from Sunday's leftovers. A large joint of meat was cooked on Sundays with plenty of vegetables. We had cold meat and pickles for Sunday tea, with homemade cakes and sometimes either tinned or stewed fruit. For dinner on

Mondays we had what was left of the meat, sliced, with 'bubble and squeak', in which the leftover vegetables from the Sunday dinner were mixed with mashed potatoes and pressed into a frying pan to form what looked like a very large pancake. When it was cooked very slowly, it really did 'bubble and squeak', blowing up pockets of air which exploded like small volcanoes. It was a simple, tasty and easy meal to cook.

Sunday dinner was the most important meal of the week. My father insisted on good behaviour at the dinner table, as he wanted to enjoy his dinner in peace. Talking had to be kept to a minimum. I was a terrible chatterbox, I could never contain myself and I usually ended up being sent to the kitchen to eat on my own in silence. If I wanted a second helping, I knocked on the door and pushed my plate forward to ask for more, I only had to catch my sister's eye to send me off into a fit of giggles, so back to the kitchen I went with my plate. I tried very hard to keep quiet, but I was always bursting with things to say. A glance at my school reports confirms the problem, a recurring comment from my teachers was, 'Doris is inclined to be talkative'. We were not allowed to leave the table when we had finished our dinner until we asked permission, and had to ask 'Please may I leave the table?'

When we had a piece of roast beef it was accompanied by Yorkshire pudding, roast potatoes, cabbage, carrots and turnips and, when they were in season, parsnips or sprouts. Carrots and turnips were chopped into small pieces, mixed, together with a nob of butter, sprinkled with pepper, and then mashed. The butcher would put a piece of white suet on top of the joint before he wrapped it up, to make the beef stay moist and succulent while it was cooking.

SCHOOL DAYS

1938

1 School photograph, taken in 1938.

Holy Baptism

As many of you as have been baptised into Christ have put on Christ *Gal 3.27*

Doris Jean

The Child of

George J. Alice Railton Hinchliffe

Was Baptised on

March 19th 1932

By Horace W Dyke Curate

At St. Luke's Church, Walton.

Ye are to take care that this Child be brought to the Bishop to be confirmed by him.

"Suffer little Children to come unto Me." "I am the Door."

"HOME WORDS" SERIES, No. 151

2 My baptism certificate.

GIRLS.

Liverpool Education Committee.

School .... Department ....

Report .... 194 3.

Standard ......

Roll ...55

Name of Scholar .... Place 4

Attendance .... Conduct ....

Scripture	Arithmetic ....
English:	Drawing ....
Reading	
Writing	Domestic Economy ......
Spelling	Needlework ....
Composition	
History	Cookery ....
Geography	Laundry ....

Remarks ....

(Signed) .... Class Teacher.
.... Head Teacher.

I have examined the Report for 19
upon the work of my daughter.
(Signed) ....

The Managers request that this slip be signed by the Parent, detached, and returned to School without delay.

3 My school report from 1943.

4 Me, aged ten, as Oberon and Jean Davies as Titania,
in a performance of *A Midsummer Night's Dream*
in Walton Hall Park.

5 My father with his pipe, walking
stick and newspaper, by the sand
dunes on Ainsdale Beach.

6 Me, aged three, with Teddy.

7 'Me' on Blundellsands Beach.

8 My sister Joyce and I on horseback at Southport Beach.

9 Left to right: Ronnie Greig, Joyce and me, on Crosby Beach.

10 My father flanked by me and Joyce.

11 On the seafront at Waterloo, in the Rock Garden with my father and Joyce.

12 Our woollen 'bumble bee' bathing costumes.

13 My mother (middle) with friends at Neston on the Wirral, around 1916.

14 My father with friends at the time they were called up in January 1916; one was killed, my father lost a leg, and two came home safely.

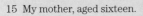
15 My mother, aged sixteen.

16 My mother, aged
eighteen, with her new,
modern hairstyle.

17 My mother outside her parents' house.

18 Auntie Elsie's and Uncle Bill's wedding, 1916. Uncle Bill later served in the Merchant Navy on the Arctic Convoys.

19 My parents' wedding, 24th February 1929. This photo is so much of its time. My father's mother Phoebe is seated in the front row on the left of the picture; my father's sister, Alice, is standing in the middle row, second from the left; Uncle Harry is behind my father in the centre; my grandfather on my mother's side is in the middle row on the right, my grandmother in front of him; Auntie Elsie is standing in the top right of the picture, holding baby Margaret.

20 & 21 My parents on board the ferry to the Isle of Man on their honeymoon, summer 1929.

22 My mother on her honeymoon, looking at Laxey Wheel, on the Isle of Man.

23 Bon voyage! The family on the *Duchess of Bedford*, 1938.

24 Cheers! My father, Uncle Sam, Uncle George and his son, Ernest, on the *Duchess of Bedford*, 1938

25 Uncle Sam's sister, second from the left, looking like Wallis Simpson, on the *Duchess of Bedford*, 1938

26 My father's sister, Alice.

27 Auntie Emma, the pianist.

28 Betty and Syd at their wedding at Caxton Hall in West London, 1948.

29 Auntie Margaret, the knitter.

CITY OF LIVERPOOL
JUNIOR CITY SCHOLARSHIP EXAMINATION,
FRIDAY, 5th MARCH, 1943.

2134

Candidate's Number................................ R ....

Name ....Hinchliffe, Doris Joan.............

Elementary School ....Arnot St...............

Place of Examination.

Read very carefully the Instructions on the other side.

P.22955. 529.

The Subjects of the Examinations will be taken as follows :—

FRIDAY, 5th MARCH.

    9.30 to 10.15—Arithmetic.

    10.30 to 11.15—English.

    11.30 to 12.5 —General Test.

Candidates must be present at the Examination Centre not later than 9.10 a.m. Those ... g later than the time named may be excluded from the Examination.

Candidates should bring with them their w pens, penc., india rubbers and no ooks or papers. Writing paper ng will be provided.

30 My exam card, front and back

31 Me, aged ten.

32 Me and my friend Barbara
with our tennis racquets at
Queen Mary High School.

To go with the meat and vegetables, we had Colman's mustard and either horseradish sauce or bread and butter pickle. I liked the bread and butter pickle, it was simply cucumber and onion sliced into vinegar and left to stand for a few hours. I used to enjoy it in sandwiches the next day when the vinegar had really soaked in.

Roast leg or shoulder of lamb was eaten with roast potatoes and either carrots and turnip, cabbage, or fresh garden peas, when they were in season. The mint sauce we had with the lamb was made with freshly chopped mint, vinegar and a teaspoon of sugar, and it was marvellous for piling onto the cabbage to disguise the taste.

Roast pork was my favourite, with the roast potatoes, cauliflower and seasonal broad beans, we had lashings of apple sauce and stuffing, which was never made from a packet, it was always homemade. Because the pork had been liberally sprinkled and rubbed with salt, the fat under the crackling on the top of the pork turned golden brown and crispy. We were given a strip of the fluffy, tasty crackling to eat.

We could tell the seasons by the vegetables we ate. Spring cabbage started to appear in March, broad beans came in early summer and only had a short season, so too did the fresh garden peas. My sister and I were given the job of shelling the peas and beans into a basin. We enjoyed doing this, as the peas were so sweet and tasty; I used to eat quite a few while I was shelling them. The broad beans lay snugly in their large green furry lined pods. Sprouts were a winter vegetable and appeared in time for Christmas. With chestnuts, sprouts were an essential part of Christmas dinner, although I didn't really like them, they were so much like small cabbages. Now, I really enjoy them.

For pudding we had apple pie and custard, or rice pudding made with evaporated milk to give it a rich creamy texture. Before it was put in the oven, the mixture was topped with butter and sprinkled liberally with nutmeg. During baking, a nutmeg-flavoured skin formed on top of the pudding. I liked the rice pudding but hated the skin.

Sometimes if there was enough stale bread, we had bread and butter pudding. Fresh bread was bought or delivered daily, because it went stale very quickly. There were two versions of bread and butter pudding. One was made with buttered slices of bread scattered with sultanas, layered in a dish, covered with custard, and then baked in the oven. For the other one, the bread was cut into small pieces mixed with dried fruit and a sprinkling of mixed spice, then bound together with milk and a beaten egg to give it a smooth consistency, like a cake mixture. It was baked in the oven in a cake tin, and we had it hot with custard, or when it was cool, we would cut it into slices to eat. We made toast either under the grill or by holding the bread in front of the fire with a toasting fork. My favourite pudding of all was steamed jam pudding with custard, which we had mainly during the really cold winter months.

Christmas dinner was special, we had a piece of pork and either a 'capon' chicken, or a turkey. A 'capon' chicken was a male bird which had a hormone pellet inserted under its skin giving it female characteristics, it became plump and tender and squatted down trying to lay eggs. Chicken was a luxury and eaten on special occasions.

When we had a turkey, it was my mother's Christmas present from her sister Lizzie, whose husband had a butcher's shop. The fresh turkey appeared on Christmas Eve with its head and some of its white feathers still on its neck, and worst of all it had to have all its giblets (heart, kidneys, liver etc.) pulled from its body. I couldn't bear to watch as they made a horrible sucking sound when they came out. My mother inspected them carefully, opening the gall bladder to see if it was a good healthy bird, then she set aside the giblets to make stock for the gravy. Christmas dinner was never quite the same after I'd seen all the preparations.

Preparations for Christmas began as early as September with the ritual making of the Christmas puddings. When the final ingredients, a bottle of stout and some tiny silver threepenny bits had been mixed in, we all had a quick stir and made a wish. The mixture was enough for three puddings, one for Christmas day, one for Boxing Day, and one for New Year's Day. Covered in greaseproof paper then wrapped and tied tightly with a clean piece of white cotton cloth, the puddings were steamed, one by one, for eight hours over a couple of days in the large iron pan, making the kitchen walls run with steam.

Once the puddings were cooked, it was time to gather the ingredients for the Christmas cake and the bun loaf. The Christmas cake was a rich, dark, fruit cake containing rum, that was baked in a round tin. Once cool, it was carefully wrapped in waxed paper, layers of brown paper and left to mature in a large cake tin. A couple of weeks before Christmas, the cake was brought out to be decorated with marzipan and icing. I love marzipan and my mother made a bit extra for me to eat while I 'helped'. When the marzipan had set, the cake was covered with royal icing and 'Merry Xmas' was carefully piped on in red by my mother. A small robin and some tiny bunches of holly, saved from previous years, were placed in the centre. To finish off, a shiny red and gold frilly band from Blackler's was wrapped around the cake and tied with a red satin ribbon. The bun loaf was a fairly basic fruitcake recipe, laced with sherry, baked in an oblong tin and left plain without marzipan or icing, with semicircles of crystallised angelica on top for decoration.

My mother made plenty of jams and bottled fruit. Plums, damsons and blackcurrants made really good jam, because they had plenty of pectin and set easily. I stood and watched my mother skim the stones off the boiling plum and damson mixtures with a slotted spoon. As the mixture simmered and bubbled they slowly rose to the surface. This was something I was not allowed to help with, as the hot jam mixture was dangerous and could easily cause a nasty burn if mishandled.

My mother would put some of the stones on a saucer for me, and after they had cooled down I would suck on them, like sweets. This was also the best way to test whether or not the jam had reached setting point; if the surface of the small blobs of jam in the saucer wrinkled when pushed, the jam was ready. Once the jam had reached setting point it was poured immediately into the prepared, warmed jam jars, sealed with waxed paper discs, then a lid was screwed firmly in place.

For bottling fruit, Kilner jars were washed and then heated in the oven to sterilise them. The fruit was cleaned, washed and carefully packed into the Kilner jars as tightly as possible, then pushed down with the handle of a wooden spoon. A hot sugar and water syrup was poured into each jar, right to the top, before it was sealed quickly with a screw top to create a vacuum. The bottled fruit was used in fruit pies, crumbles and cobblers during the winter months.

The bottled tomatoes made sure my father could have fried tomatoes in winter with his weekend hearty breakfasts of bacon and egg. Sometimes he had dried salt cod on Sunday mornings, which had to be soaked overnight on Saturday. It was rather strange and looked just like a piece of cardboard. His favourite fish was smoked haddock.

Whatever happened to the beautiful fresh English fruits that were plentiful in summer and autumn? Deep-purple Victoria plums, covered in a fine bloom, a gentle squeeze ensured that when you bit into the plum, the stone came cleanly away, leaving only the sweet golden flesh. Yellow egg plums had a distinctive colour and scented flavour. The last time I saw some really luscious damsons was a few years ago, on holiday in Germany with my husband and son. Driving through the Saarland on a very hot day, we stopped just off the roadside for a picnic under a large, gnarled old tree, the only shade we could find. As we sat and ate our picnic, things began to plop down gently on the car and we realised we were sitting under a damson tree.

A treat I loved in summer was a bag of ripe cherries from the greengrocer. Plentiful and cheap, they were rich, dark red and so juicy that it was difficult to stop the juice from running down my chin, where it would drip and leave a bright red stain on my clothes and fingers. The cherries had to be eaten quickly otherwise the bottom would fall out of the brown paper bag because they were so juicy.

On Tuesdays, my mother did housework in the mornings and then went shopping in the afternoons. She had two wicker shopping baskets. The brown one was large, round and deep with a strong looped handle, this one was used for heavy items such as vegetables and fruit. The basket was lined with newspaper, to stop any soil from falling through when the potatoes were tipped into it from a metal scoop. The rest of the vegetables and fruit were put in, with the fruit on top in brown paper bags. The other basket was much smaller, and was light cream, rectangular in shape and decorated with brightly coloured raffia flowers. This one was kept for bread, cakes, eggs and smaller items of shopping, such as sausages and cooked meats.

My mother was a very good plain cook and only used fresh ingredients. Here are some examples of what we could expect to have:

MONDAY This was the day when we used up the food left over from Sunday. Vegetables, cold meats and apple pie.

TUESDAY Grilled lamb chops, vegetables and roast potatoes.

WEDNESDAY Steak and kidney pie, or shepherd's pie with mashed potatoes and vegetables.

THURSDAY Smoked fillet of haddock with bacon and poached eggs, or liver, onions and bacon with mashed potato.

FRIDAY Grilled ham and chips, or steaks of cod or hake, with mashed potatoes and peas.

SATURDAY Hotpot or casserole, placed in the oven to cook very slowly for a few hours.

Puddings varied from day to day, according to what fruit was available at the greengrocers.

On Saturday afternoons, my mother, my sister and I would go shopping and my father would go for a drink with his friends.

The hotpot could be eaten whenever we were ready to dip into it. Puddings were usually apple pie, stewed fruit, apple crumble or a fruit cobbler. There were many other dishes but these were the staples.

A teatime treat on a Saturday was a box of cakes from Cooper's, a shop which sold the most delicious Rum Babas, Cream Pyramids, Cream Slices, Cream Horns and my favourite – large meringues. We occasionally had some of these on a weekday if my mother had not had time to bake.

Only two types of coffee were available: Camp coffee and ground coffee. Instant coffee was not yet available. Camp coffee was sold in tall thin bottles, like sauce bottles, and it looked and tasted like treacle. It had a very distinctive label; an Indian soldier wearing a multi-coloured turban, standing in front of a seated soldier in a Scot's uniform, holding out a tray on which there was a bottle of coffee. On this bottle was a picture of an Indian soldier holding a tray with a bottle of coffee, on which there was a picture of an Indian ... I remember looking at this bottle and thinking 'This could go on forever!'

Cooper's sold many varieties of ground coffee. In the side window of the shop, a man dressed in a white uniform with a tall white hat worked the machines which roasted and ground the coffee beans. The tantalising whiffs of coffee outside drew you into the shop, and once inside your nostrils were assailed with the smell of roasting coffee.

At home, my mother prepared coffee in a large blue and white willow patterned jug. Once the coffee and hot water were in, the jug was covered with a circle of fine mesh cloth which had heavy china beads sewn around the edge, this served as a strainer for the coffee, and I still have one as a keepsake. Cooper's was a large city centre grocer's shop which sold some very unusual and exotic foods, with a section of foods for the Chinese community and another section set aside for Kosher foods to cater for the Jewish community.

❖❖❖

When my mother and father married, my grandparents gave them, as wedding presents, their piano and my grandmother's sewing machine. Many houses had a piano, and it was quite a status symbol. My grandmother had diabetes and her sight was beginning to deteriorate, so she and my grandfather were going to live with my mother's eldest sister, Elsie, who had a large house with four double bedrooms. With three children to look after and Uncle Bill away for long periods in the Merchant Navy, Elsie was glad of the companionship. Sadly, I don't remember my grandmother. She died from the effects of her diabetes eighteen months after I was born.

I remember my grandfather though. He died aged seventy-six, when I was six years old. He had thick silvery hair and a small beard, and he was still living with Auntie Elsie. Whenever we went to visit, we would pop upstairs to sit on grandpa's bed and listen to one of his stories, mostly about his life and his childhood. He was born and grew up in Charrington Street, London, leaving home when he was twenty years old. Now, in his old age, he was confined to his room because he'd had to have part of his leg amputated. When he'd finished his story, with a beaming smile he'd ask us to go to the small middle drawer in the big chest of drawers in the corner of his room, and pass him his tin of tobacco, so he could smoke his pipe. There was always a small bag of sweets sitting alongside the tin of tobacco, either Dolly Mixtures or Jelly Babies.

Grandpa's room was next to the bathroom at the end of a long landing. After he died, whenever I had to use the bathroom I sped past the door of the room which had once been his and where he had died. Death is a frightening thing for small children. In those days the body was brought home and the coffin was set on a stand in the sitting room. Neighbours and friends came in and out to view the corpse and pay their respects. They stood around the coffin, sipping a strong drink, remembering the time they had spent together. I remember being asked if I wanted to kiss grandpa goodbye. I fled!

I have two photographs of my grandmother, one taken at my Auntie Elsie's wedding in 1916, and another taken at my mother's wedding in 1929. In the photograph of 1916, Elsie, the bride, wore a full-length dress of lace with a heavy lace veil. Her younger sisters were the bridesmaids, and they wore Edwardian-style outfits. The dresses were long-waisted with pleated skirts, and they wore straw boaters with long velvet ribbons hanging down the back. My grandmother wore a long silk taffeta dress with lots of pin tucks and leg-of-mutton sleeves. Round the waist of the dress is what appears to be a heavily fringed apron in matching material.

Comparing the wedding photographs of 1916 and 1929, the change in the fashions and the effect it had on the people who wore them is quite remarkable. In 1929, my mother is wearing a flapper-style wedding dress made of white satin, coming just below the knee, with an overskirt of dozens and dozens of strings of small silver glass beads. Round her neck is a white satin choker with a small spray of wax orange blossom. The bridesmaids are wearing fine, light-coloured silk dresses and cloche hats, with a large floppy rose for decoration. They are all wearing white pure silk stockings and white satin shoes with Louis heels. My grandmother, who now appears younger in the 1929 photograph than she did in 1916, is very stylishly dressed in a short two-tone chiffon dress with a matching coat, fine silk stockings and shoes with heels.

Music played a pivotal part in providing entertainment in my grandparents' home. Every Saturday evening my grandmother kept open house for friends and relatives. When Grandpa came home from work on Saturday nights he was usually very merry, having had a few drinks on the way home. He always sang his favourite song, 'Little Brown Jug', accompanied by the piano.

My mother and father were very pleased to have the piano, even though neither of them could play. It was made of figured walnut, with inlaid, coloured, marquetry panels of flowers, and heavy brass candlesticks at each end which swivelled from side to side. One of my mother's friends was a music teacher, so my sister and I took music lessons once a week, at a cost of 1s 6d an hour. We learnt the names of the notes, practised the correct fingering and scales and over a period of time we also learnt to play some pleasant little tunes. We even sat for a few beginners exams, but after a while it became obvious that we just did not have enough musical talent to carry on further with the lessons.

My mother's sister, Emma, had a surprising musical gift. She'd never had a piano lesson but she only had to hear a snippet of a tune then she could play it. She played everything 'by ear'. When anyone asked Emma, 'Emma do you know this tune?' her reply was, 'How does it go? Hum it to me.' She sat at the piano and picked it out, slowly at first, but once she got the hang of it, she was off.

The sewing machine was always in use. In my grandmother's house it had served the family well for many years, before it came to my mother. Nearly all the clothes for the children, the soft furnishings and household repairs were done on it. My grandmother had help with the sewing and every Tuesday a neighbour, who needed a bit of extra cash, came in to do some sewing. As well as a small payment she was given a bottle of gin, which she drank steadily while she sewed. She never had any patterns; she just held the material up to each child, then ripped or cut the material to shape, taking pins from her mouth as she did so to hold the material in place. Fortified by the gin, she sewed like fury, turning out many lovely outfits.

On Wednesday afternoons, when the shops were shut, my mother sewed. Once any repairs and darning were completed, she turned her attention to making things. Cushion covers, pinafores, curtains, many of her own clothes and all of mine and my sister's clothes were made on this wonderful old Singer sewing machine. Our dresses were made from 'Miss Muffet' cotton print material, with gathered waists, puff sleeves and Peter Pan collars. Not only were the dresses made in this material, but we also had matching knickers.

Princess Elizabeth and Princess Margaret Rose were just a little bit older than my sister and me, and at the time, the two princesses set the trend for children's fashions. Everyone wanted their daughters to look like the little princesses. We were able to do this because Weldons, the pattern firm, sold paper patterns of their clothes. We had coats and hats just like the ones worn by Elizabeth and Margaret. My 'princess' outfit was in a fine misty blue tweed and my sister's was a light tan colour.

In 1938, my mother's brother, Sam, who had emigrated to America with his family some years earlier in 1923, came home for a visit, bringing with him his wife, his mother-in-law and his two sisters-in-law. When the time came for him to return to America, all the family went on board the ship, the Duchess of Bedford, to see them off. I have a photograph of my sister and myself resplendent in our new coats and hats, sitting with all the female members of the family who had gone to say goodbye. The men had a separate photograph taken of themselves drinking a farewell toast. With all the excitement of the bands playing on the dock and people waving, we really thought we were princesses.

I remember experiencing a dreadful moment of panic when a man came onto the loudspeaker system, telling anyone not travelling to leave the ship, 'All ashore who's going ashore', he announced. No one seemed to take any notice for a while and I was convinced we would all end up in America! Soon after they went home to Los Angeles, the war started and we lost touch, we never saw the family again. I have recently been doing research on our family history and I found out that my Uncle Sam died in 1943, aged fifty-five, still in Los Angeles.

Looking at the photographs, it's noticeable how very slim and elegant the Americans look. Uncle Sam's sister, in fact, looks just like Wallis Simpson, the infamous American divorcee whose relationship with Edward VIII caused a constitutional crisis, ending with his abdication. She was also famous for saying 'No woman can be too rich or too thin'.

I spent many happy hours learning to sew on grandma's treadle machine, which was kept in my parents' house in the corner of the dining room by the window. It was very solid and reliable and quite easy to use. First of all, under my mother's watchful eye, I learnt how to control the treadle with my feet. I practised making patterns on pieces of paper, with no thread in the needle, then I learnt to thread the needle and shuttle correctly. I progressed to making dolls' clothes, then some dressing up and party outfits for me and my friends, mostly made from crêpe paper. Finally, from about the age of twelve, I went on to make my own clothes.

The best and most memorable thing I made on this machine was my wedding dress in 1954. Made from white slipper satin with a yoke and sleeves of lace, trimmed with seed pearls, it was a labour of love. I just don't know how any house can function without a sewing machine. My sewing machine now is electric, and at the flick of a switch will do buttonholes, embroidery and invisible hemming!

❖❖❖

Once a fortnight, my mother treated herself to a trip to the hairdresser's for a shampoo and set. After her hair had been washed, thick green Palmolive setting lotion was poured onto her hair and the waves were carefully pushed and pressed into place by the fingers of the hairdresser. When the lotion set, her hair was as stiff as a board. This style of deep waving was called a 'Marcel Wave'.

Sometimes my mother had a 'hot' wave. Curling tongs were heated on a long thin gas burner, and when the tongs were hot enough, they were opened and the ends of the hair were trapped inside. The curling tongs were then twisted around, holding the hair, creating tight curls and waves. The hairdressers also did singeing. After a haircut, a long thin taper was lit and then passed quickly over the ends of the hair to seal them. The overriding smell in the hairdresser's shop was of hot burning hair, mixed with the sickly smell of the setting lotion. All the hairdressers in ladies' salons were women; it was a place for women only. Men went to the barber's for a 'short back and sides'.

When my sister and I needed to have our hair cut, my mother took us to Lewis's department store, which had a hairdressing salon specifically for children. There were high swivel chairs in the form of animals and you could pick which animal you wanted to sit on. There was a panda, a duck, a giraffe, a tiger, a penguin and a lion. The panda was the favourite one, not least because of the famous panda named Ming in the London Zoo.

As well as getting her hair done, my mother enjoyed her occasional trips to the afternoon tea dances at Francis and McKay's, which were held in the room above the cake shop. This was a lovely cake shop and restaurant, where the waitresses wore black dresses, white frilly aprons and caps. All the cakes were made on the premises and right in the centre of the shop window, on display, was a magnificent example of one of their three-tiered wedding cakes. It stood on an ornate silver stand and on the top tier of cake, a small bride and groom stood beneath an archway covered in tiny white flowers. My mother went with her friend and sometimes, if I was off school, I had to accompany her and sit quietly, whilst they danced to the music of the three-piece band. The instruments were a piano, a violin and an accordion, which were all played by women.

Most of the dancers were women, as their husbands were at work. The few husbands who were there danced with their wives. To me, they all looked quite old, like grandparents. The dances were held during summer afternoons, for some reason which I did not understand, the ladies wore their summer hats and white gloves while they danced. After coming down from the dance hall in the small shaky metal lift which looked like a cage, on our way out we had to pass round the back of the wedding cake, at which point, I always had an irresistible desire to push the cake over. I was sure my mother could read my mind, because when she caught me looking at the cake, she would fix me with one of her looks, which usually meant, 'Don't even think about it young lady.'

Hats were very important to women, even in the summer most ladies wore hats. My mother rarely went out without her hat. There was always a couple of milliners shops in any shopping area, providing a very good selection of the latest styles. The assistant could change the decoration on any hat to suit the taste of the customer, with a new piece of Petersham ribbon, different flowers, or feathers. Also, if a felt hat was too tight it could be stretched in the shop while you waited, on a large wooden head-shaped block. When winter turned into spring, it was a good excuse for lots of women to buy a new hat.

For those who couldn't afford a new hat, one from the previous year was brought out and refurbished with new ribbons, net, or sprays of silk flowers. Sometimes small bunches of fruit were used, particularly shiny red cherries. For summer, my mother liked one in a fine light straw, which was a change from the heavy dark felt hats that she had worn during the winter. The new hats usually came out for the first time on Easter Sunday, either for church or if the weather was fine, for a stroll in the park.

Next door to Francis & McKay's was a small family-run department store called Brown's, which catered only for women. They sold millinery, gloves, scarves, handbags, handkerchiefs, stockings, underwear, nightdresses and their speciality, Spirella corsets. They were made of thick pink cotton, stiffened with whalebone and flattened steel springs. The corsets were laced tightly up the back and fastened at the front with large hooks and eyes, set in flat steel rods. If any lady was too shy be fitted in the shop, the Spirella 'corsetiere' would make a home visit. The corsets, or 'stays' as they were sometimes called, were meant to control the figure and support the back. How women coped with these corsets, especially in summer, I just don't know. I couldn't imagine anything worse; it must have felt like being in a strait jacket.

My mother enjoyed shopping in George Henry Lee & Co., the Liverpool branch of the John Lewis Partnership, where she bought bedding, towels and dress material. They had everything for the home. Not many years later, the material for my wedding dress and the dresses for my bridesmaids would come from George Henry Lee, and my wedding cake was made by the chef in their restaurant.

Coming out of George Henry Lee's, we would often pass the 'Umbrella Man'. He had his repair shop in a narrow alleyway leading off Williamson Square into St John's Market. He could repair or refurbish any umbrella with a new black fabric cover – umbrellas were nearly always black then – new spokes, a new handle, a new elastic fastener, and fit a new ferrule on the tip. The Umbrella Man was very tall and thin, with a gaunt face. When he was not in the shop, he wore a long black gaberdine overcoat which flapped in the wind as he strode along carrying a folded umbrella. He looked like a half-open umbrella. I thought he was a wizard of some sort.

Each Christmas, near to his shop, puppy cages stood on handcarts beneath gas burners. Groups of new puppies shivered with the cold, huddling together for warmth. The puppies were all mongrels, bred to be sold as Christmas presents by poor people who lived around Scotland Road. The puppy-sellers were mainly Irish, they wore homemade black woollen shawls and they too shivered with the cold. There was a special police fund set up to provide shoes for the barefoot children of Scotland Road. The area was heavily bombed during the war and most of the houses were destroyed, with only the pubs left standing on the corner of each road.

Where we lived, the butcher, the baker, and the grocer employed delivery boys, who rode on sturdy black bicycles with large wicker baskets resting on specially made handlebars. My mother's weekly grocery order came from a shop called Irwin's, but she also had to go shopping during the week. I enjoyed going shopping with my mother for groceries. The grocer's shop was double-fronted, with the door set back in the centre. The front was painted maroon, with the name of the shop 'Irwin's' painted on it in gold lettering. The floor of the entrance to the shop was made from small, black and white, diamond-shaped marble tiles. On the door was a big brass handle with a thumb latch, which I had to reach up and press to go in.

In the shop we were served by a male assistant who wore a white cotton coat. Many foodstuffs were stored in bulk and were quite heavy to move. The wrapping and folding of the packing of the groceries was fun to watch. The sugar was weighed out and then poured, from a scoop, into dark blue paper bags, labelled with TATE & LYLE and the weight in black letters. The bags varied in size according to the weight they were to hold – half a pound, one pound, two pounds. The assistant folded the top of the bags over before securing the corners neatly.

Butter was taken from a big mound kept on a white marble slab, to keep it cool. Chunks were scooped off with square wooden paddles and weighed to the customer's requirements. The butter was then shaped into oblongs, using the wooden paddles. Finally, patterned paddles were used, leaving an imprint in the butter. The paddles had carved patterns on them, such as leaves, or even the word 'butter'. Sometimes a mould bearing a cow was pressed into the top of the butter to give further decoration, before it was neatly wrapped, first in waxed greaseproof paper and then a brown paper bag.

Most biscuits didn't come ready-wrapped in fancy packages. They were sold by weight from large, square, shiny red tins, with glass tops so the biscuits could be clearly seen. The tins were presented on ledges, which tipped them forwards slightly, so the variety in each tin was easy to recognise. To keep them fresh, the lids were always tightly closed and each layer was separated by a sheet of corrugated greaseproof paper. You could make your own mix, by picking a few from each tin, to the weight you required. Broken biscuits were put to one side in a separate tin and sold off very cheaply. Sometimes, if I gave the man serving us a nice smile and he was in a good mood, he would give me a small white paper bag of 'brokens'.

Bacon was sliced on a large red and silver machine, and came in whole sides, either smoked or unsmoked. From these sides the customer would order rashers of streaky, best back, or whole rashers, the desired thickness of each rasher, and the number of slices. The bacon was firmly wrapped in greaseproof paper. Plastic bags and cling film were not yet in use.

Big round blocks of cheese, encased in coarse, often mouldy looking cotton cloth, sat on blocks of cool white marble. The cheese was cut with either a very large sharp knife or a strong piece of wire with a wooden spindle across the end, to pull it through the cheese. The customer would say a little bit more, or a little bit less as the assistant guided the cutter across the cheese, pointing to the right amount to be cut.

The same assistant would serve you all of your items, moving round the shop with you from counter to counter. As you went around he would write down the cost of each item on a paper pad of bills, which bore the name of the shop at the top, before finally adding up the items and presenting you with the bill. He would then pack your basket carefully for you, with the heavy packets at the bottom and the more fragile things on top.

Shopping was a leisurely process, not something that could be hurried as you went from shop to shop. Most fresh items had to be bought on a daily basis, going to different shops for vegetables, groceries, bread, meat, fish and cakes. Things such as firelighters, paraffin oil, bundles of firewood, polish and candles came from the chandler's.

When we reached home, there was the excitement of being allowed to unpack the basket and help to put all the items in their proper places, either in the 'meat safe', a wooden cupboard in the kitchen with a wire mesh grill over the front for foodstuffs which needed some air, or in the storage cupboard for dry goods, alongside the kitchen range.

My husband was a Londoner, and in 1956 we bought our first car, an Austin A30. We took my mother to London to show her the sights which, until then, she had only heard about. We drove into Downing Street, turned round at the end, and parked outside Number 10. In those days the world was a simpler, safer place, and we had more freedom. The young policeman on duty outside Number 10 had been watching us carefully, and he came over and said, 'Hello, you're a long way from home, what are you doing here?' We were surprised, because we didn't think we'd done anything wrong. The sharp-eyed young policeman had recognised the Liverpool registration letters on the car. Then, as we talked, we found out to our amazement that he was none other than the delivery boy from Irwin's who had delivered our groceries! He had moved to London to join the police force, something which my mother was very thrilled by and couldn't wait to go home to tell her friends. The world was indeed a very small place.

One thing I remember very clearly about my childhood and growing up was that my mother was always there when I came home from school, ready with a sandwich, an apple or a drink, to tide me over until my father came home from work. She was never too busy to stop and listen to what I'd done during my day at school. On the odd occasion when she was a little late coming back from shopping or a visit to a friend and wasn't in the house, I felt a slight feeling of panic.

My mother had to go into hospital for a hernia operation. She had suffered the pain for some time and it was finally decided an operation was necessary. The operation wasn't too serious and she was only in hospital for ten days. During the week we had improvised meals, but my father decided he would make sure we had a good Sunday dinner. He bought a joint of meat and took charge of its cooking, my sister peeled and cooked the vegetables; my job was to make the gravy. I had watched my mother make gravy so many times I was convinced I knew exactly what to do. Unfortunately, I misjudged the amount of Bisto and cornflour to use. I put the gravy in the gravy boat then proudly took it to the table, but when my father lifted the gravy boat to pour some over his dinner nothing happened, it had set into a solid lump. We had to tip it out onto a plate and cut it into squares. For some time afterwards I was constantly teased and reminded of my efforts at gravy making.

❖❖

My mother loved going to the cinema because it took her into another world of elegant, smartly dressed, glamorous women and romantic heroes. She took my sister and me once or twice a week. Films ran for three days, from Monday to Wednesday, before they were changed for Thursday to Saturday. Technicolor films were just coming in and were very popular, she particularly liked the spectacular musicals starring Betty Grable and Alice Faye.

I loved the films about animals, especially the ones starring Elizabeth Taylor with Lassie the collie dog, and National Velvet, where she rode a racehorse in the Grand National. I was fascinated by Elizabeth Taylor, with her hyacinth blue eyes and raven-black hair she looked so beautiful. I was born on the same day as her and I wondered why the good fairy had ignored me – why couldn't I look like that?

Two films were shown at each session; the main 'A' film and a shorter 'B' film, which were advertisements for local traders and trailers of forthcoming attractions that were shown during the interval. There was always an up-to-date newsreel by Pathé, keeping us informed of world events.

In the interval when the lights came on, we had a chance to buy an ice cream or sweets from the usherette, who walked around carrying a large wooden tray held in place by a strap over her shoulder. In large cinemas an organ decorated with coloured lights came up from below the stage and played popular tunes to entertain the audience while they ate their sweets and ice creams.

My mother's favourite sweets were marrons glacés, which she bought at Christmas for a treat, and sugared almonds. When we went to Southport to shop, she bought some sugared almonds from Matti & Tissot, to remind her of the times when she and my father were courting in the 1920s. They went into Matti & Tissot for afternoon tea and my father always bought some for her to take home.

Some years ago, Matti & Tissot closed down because the younger members of the family no longer wanted to carry on with the business. Everything was put up for sale. I bought one of the silver-plated tea and coffee sets bearing their name, made especially for the café by Mappin & Webb. Who knows, it may have been one used by my parents nearly eighty years ago?

Chapter Nine

MY FATHER

My father, George James, was one of six children, Wilfred, Alice, George, Nora, Phoebe and Edith. He was born on 12th December 1897, the year of Queen Victoria's Diamond Jubilee. He was always called Jim by everyone who knew him, and he was both a gentle man and a gentleman. I remember his fair hair, his blue eyes and his perfect set of teeth. When I look at pictures of him, it is just like seeing me looking back at me.

When he was young, one of the things he really enjoyed was to go fishing with his father on the river Dee near Chester, especially at a pub overlooking the river called The Cross Keys. In January 1916, he was conscripted into the Army, the King's Liverpool Rifles, and was sent off to fight in the battlefields of Flanders. In terrible fighting in the Ypres Salient, a shell landed behind him, blowing his left leg apart below the knee. He told us that he would have died if it hadn't been for the quick thinking of his sergeant, who punched him to the ground and stayed with him until medical help arrived. He was taken to a field hospital staffed by Australian doctors and nurses, where his leg was amputated just below the knee. He had nothing but praise for the care and attention that he received from them in appalling circumstances. After two years and one hundred and thirty-three days he was discharged from the army, pronounced 'unfit for service'.

I once remarked to my husband how sad it was that my father's young life had been so badly affected by this, and my husband replied thoughtfully that if he hadn't lost his leg he might have gone into another battle and lost his life. If that had happened, I wouldn't be here.

My father was a man of remarkable courage and determination, who worked until he was sixty-five years of age. Thirty-eight years of his life were spent in the offices of local government, providing for and supporting his family, taking only four weeks off sick in all those years. At the end of his working life he duly received an illuminated certificate and a clock to mark his years of service. The clock was always stopping and never kept very good time. My father was never really happy in retirement; he missed the company of his colleagues at work and the feelings of being busy and useful.

Before my parents' marriage, my mother's sister, Elsie, tried to persuade her not to marry my father. She said, 'You'll be a nursemaid to him all your married life and probably a young widow.' Happily, my mother paid no heed to the warning. She loved my father and the wedding went ahead as planned, with my mother stylishly dressed in her 1920s flapper-style dress and my father cutting a dash in his black suit, a shirt with a winged collar and a grey felt hat.

He did not forgive Elsie for her remark, and he never went to her family New Year's Eve parties. Stubbornly, he went on to outlive Elsie, her husband, and all of my mother's sisters and their husbands. Although we hardly knew my father's brothers and sisters – none of them lived locally – we found out gradually over the years that he had managed to outlive them also. I am sure his long life was due not only to his dogged determination, but also to my mother's loving care and attention for so many years.

My father never wanted to talk about his time in Flanders, it was very much a closed subject, at least to me and my sister, and he probably only confided in my mother. Sometimes he woke up in the night very upset, having had dreadful nightmares. The horrific things he had seen on the battlefield must have been deep in his subconscious. One thing he did tell us was that he felt he could still wiggle the toes on his left foot.

The only times he became upset and showed deep emotion about his time in the trenches was when he heard the songs 'Pack up Your Troubles' and 'The Roses of Picardy'. These two songs moved him to tears, and whenever he tried to sing them he had to give up, the memories were too difficult to cope with.

When war was declared in September 1939, his comment was 'Thank heavens I have no sons to provide the politicians with more cannon fodder'. He did complain occasionally of the injustice of the pension system, where 'other ranks' received a relatively meagre pension for the same injury as an officer; after all, each leg was equally important to its owner. He never let this bitterness last for long and stoically got on with his life.

My sister and I didn't think it was unusual to have a father with an artificial limb. It was there and we accepted it as part of him. When he was a young man, he walked so well, most people thought he just had a slight limp. He was very nippy at jumping on and off a moving tram or bus. When other children started to boast about what their fathers did and what they had, my boast that my father had an artificial leg partly made of wood was a trump card which stopped them dead in their tracks. Occasionally, I would ask one of them in to see this phenomenon. My father would patiently roll up his trouser leg a little way to give them a quick glimpse and a brave child would tap the leg gently to see if it really was made of wood.

My love of reading came from my father. Every week I would go with him to the public library, and sometimes to the small Atlas private library where they had lots of second-hand books and new Book Club books, which were cheap editions of popular publications. They made a small charge for each book borrowed. When I got my juniors ticket to the main library, I read and cried over: Anna Sewell's *Black Beauty*, *Anne of Green Gables*, Louisa May Alcott's *Little Women* and *Jo's Boys*, *What Katy Did*, Charles Kingsley's *The Water Babies*, Kenneth Grahame's *The Wind in the Willows*, Lewis Carroll's *Alice in Wonderland* and many more, too numerous to mention here. I also enjoyed reading the Biggles books, about the daring adventures of young men in their flying machines.

When I got my library ticket for the senior section I didn't know where to start, so I picked an author, read as many of their books as I could find, and then went on to another author, for example, Jack London, E. Laurie Long, H. Ryder Haggard, Wilkie Collins, Georgette Heyer, John Galsworthy, Dorothy L. Sayers, P.G. Wodehouse, Raymond Chandler and Agatha Christie. The first book I read of Agatha Christie's was *The Hollow*, which was given to me as a present and I was hooked. Hercule Poirot and Miss Marple became my favourite detectives.

Our wireless ran on sulphuric acid batteries, square glass containers with two lead plates inside. Each battery had its own metal carrying cage with a handle, and had to be recharged once a week. The cobbler ran the battery service from the back of his shoe repair shop. I went with my father to help carry the battery as he sometimes used a walking stick. We left one battery with the cobbler, paid him sixpence to charge it, and got another battery back. When we arrived home my father connected it to the red and black terminals of the radio. It wasn't until 1943 that we were able to buy an electric wireless, an ECKO model made by EK Cole.

Sometimes I went with my father when he visited the Midland Bank. It was a stone-faced building on the corner of a road with the words 'Midland Bank' in brass letters outside. Inside there was a black and white marble floor and highly polished dark mahogany counters. The glass partitions behind the counters were made of frosted glass, so that the members of staff in the office were hidden from view. It was never very busy in the bank and people spoke very quietly. The bank clerks were all men, and I don't remember seeing any women on the counters, as they worked as clerks and typists behind the glass partitions.

When winter came, my father dreaded snow falling because it made it very difficult for him to get around, as he was unable to push off well with his left leg. In one particularly heavy snowfall, during winter in the early 1940s, the snow jammed the points on the tramway and the trams and buses stopped running. He was halfway home from work when he had to get off the tram and walk up a hill. The combination of the pressure on the foot, the depth of the snow, and the angle of the hill put too much strain on the foot of his artificial limb and the foot fell off, complete with its shoe and sock. My father just bent down, picked it up and, quite matter-of-factly, tucked it under his arm then carried on walking. The woman walking up the hill on the pavement behind him had hysterics and fainted. We thought it was very funny, but she must have had a terrible shock, poor thing.

Fortunately, he always had a spare leg in a large cardboard box, which he kept under his bed. When I first discovered the box, I was convinced it was a beautiful doll which was to be part of my Christmas present. My disappointment was very difficult to cope with when I realised what was really in the box.

Every November my father helped to organise the details, invitations and seating arrangements for the Lord Mayor's banquet in the Town Hall. Each year, as a treat, he brought my mother a slipper orchid left over from one of the floral displays. The orchid was a pale yellow-green, with brown spots and stripes. It gave off a musty smell which was not very pleasant. It sat on the sideboard in a small glass vase, with its stem wrapped in silver paper, where it managed to survive for a couple of weeks. I never did like it. I thought it was strange, exotic and quite evil, and was convinced something quite nasty was going to pop out of its 'slipper'. It wasn't a bit like any of the pretty, sweet smelling flowers I knew, and definitely not one I would have worn for decoration.

In summer my father liked to have a game of bowls. Nearby we had a small park with a good bowling green and a small pavilion. While the men played bowls the ladies made the tea and sandwiches, provided homemade cakes and had a good gossip. There was also a play area for children, with swings, a see-saw, a slide and a roundabout, surrounded by a grassy area.

In winter, my father, who was very good with his hands, made small wooden toys and spill holders, mostly in the shape of animals, which he cut out with a fretsaw. He sanded, stained and polished them to gleaming perfection. Often they were given to friends as small gifts at Christmas.

Another of his interests was stamp collecting. He had the advantage of working in a place where the letters came in from other councils and government offices all round the world. He went into the post room and cut the stamps off the envelopes before they were thrown away. On Friday nights he brought the stamps home. After the dinner things had been cleared away, he took the stamps out of his pocket and spread them on the table. Any stamps that were duplicates of those already in his collection he gave to me and my sister. We both had stamp albums given to us as Christmas presents and grew to recognise the names of countries around the world, places which we thought we would never be able to visit. I have not forgotten the names of countries as they appeared on the stamps: Helvetia (Switzerland), Magyar Posta (Hungary), Deutschland (Germany), Polska (Poland), Sverige (Sweden), Suomi (Finland) …

Collecting stamps was also a geography lesson. The stamps gave us a picture of the rest of the world, so many of the stamps came from far-away countries, bearing portraits of George V and George VI. Using our big atlas of the world we found out where the countries were, then checked to see which ones were part of the British Empire. Some were tiny places, like the Gilbert and Ellice Islands and Gibraltar; some were vast countries like Canada and Australia.

One day in 1942, my father came home with a black and white stamp, which had come into his office. The stamp was on a letter that had been in the last post to leave Singapore before it fell to the Japanese. I still have the stamp in the family collection.

The first thing my father did when he came home from work at about six o'clock was to turn on the radio and listen to the news. After his dinner he would go to sleep and wake up at exactly eight o'clock, just in time to listen to his favourite radio programme, It's That Man Again (ITMA), with Tommy Handley, and would chuckle quietly to himself at the jokes. Occasionally, just for fun, we tried really hard to make him oversleep. As eight o'clock approached, we kept absolutely quiet. Sometimes we even took the clock out of the room, moved the hands either backwards or forwards, but nothing worked. At eight o'clock on the dot he woke up. His first words when he woke up were always, 'What time is it?' Sometimes, I suspected he was awake anyway and was just pretending to be asleep to play along with our games. When he didn't listen to the radio or read, he would go out to the local. It was a social thing he did, to have a quiet drink and a chat with friends.

The one thing that was a bone of contention between my mother and father was his pipe. He would sit on the settee next to the fireplace, fill his pipe from a square gold tin of Ogden's St Bruno tobacco, his favourite brand, then press it down gently, ready to light the pipe. He lit matches, one after another, and drew air through the pipe to light it. My mother swore he smoked more matches than tobacco. Sometimes he would press the full box of matches over the bowl of the pipe to give greater suction. He threw the matches, mostly still alight, into the fire. Half of them missed the fire and fell back into the tiled fireplace. Some of them bounced out onto the hearthrug. If you sat next to him on the settee, you would have flaming matches whizzing past your nose.

Often he would fall asleep with his pipe gripped firmly between his teeth. Sometimes my mother would try to take the pipe out of his mouth in case he dropped it, but his grip on what she called his 'dummy' was like iron. As he breathed gently in and out, sparks flew out of his pipe and onto his pullover, burning small holes all over it. It looked like a pepper pot. My mother would shout: 'Jim, you're on fire!' He would wake up with a start, brush the burning ash away, smile, then go straight back to sleep. She vowed never to knit a pullover for him, refusing to spend time knitting something that was destined to go up in smoke. What he needed, she said, was an asbestos vest! The ceiling above the corner where he sat was permanently yellow with the fumes from the pipe.

Many years later, when we were taking my mother and father to visit my sister and her family in Yorkshire, we drove along with the car windows down, as it was such a lovely sunny day. We suddenly noticed a very strong, sickly smell of burning, which we thought was coming in from outside, so we wound the windows up. The smell grew stronger, so my husband stopped the car, thinking something was wrong. Nothing was wrong with the car; it was my father who was on fire. He had put his pipe, still lit, into the pocket of his new Harris Tweed sports jacket, recently bought from Dunne's. The pipe was in his left-hand pocket, above his artificial leg, and it had burnt a hole through the pocket lining of his jacket and was slowly smouldering away as it rested on the leather harness of his artificial limb. He felt nothing and smelled nothing, having slept blissfully through all the commotion. He woke up with a bewildered smile and wondered what the fuss was about.

During the Second World War, my father was in the Air Raid Precautions. He was appointed leader of the fire-watching group in our street and was issued with a grey steel helmet.

We became the proud keepers of the fire-fighting equipment: the stirrup pump, a bucket of sand and a spare bucket to fill with water. The bucket of sand was to throw straight onto fires. When the spare bucket was filled with water, the stirrup pump was put over the side; the handle of the pump was then pulled up and down while you placed your foot on the bottom plate to keep it steady. The water flowed out through the rubber hose, and the brass nozzle was well made and adjustable, giving either a wide spray or a fierce jet of water. By the time this contraption was filled with water, assembled and taken to the site of the fire, it probably would have been too late to have any effect. Fortunately, it never had to be used, but it was a comfort to have it there, just in case. The nozzle came in handy for many years afterwards, attached to my own garden hose.

❖❖❖

My father had a very good friend who had been a headmaster and was now retired. He had a good collection of books on many different subjects which he lent to my father. Most Sunday mornings my father went for a walk before he went to have a drink. On the way, he would call in to see his friend for a chat and for a while they would put the world to rights, then he would be on his way with a book under his arm. His Sunday afternoons were spent reading before he dozed off, for his 'forty winks'.

Another of my father's pleasures was listening to Gilbert and Sullivan. Before they were married, he and my mother used to go to see performances of Gilbert and Sullivan's operettas at the Lyceum Theatre on a Saturday night. The theatre closed in the 1930s, just before the war, and became derelict; it was then hit by a bomb. My father's favourite was *The Gondoliers*. I

128

remember hearing him often humming to himself, 'Take a pair of sparkling eyes, ta – ta – tum – te – tum – te – dee.'

I wish now that I had known my father better. He was a quiet man who kept his thoughts to himself. I realise now what an indomitable spirit he must have had to have kept going with very little complaint, stomping around for seventy years, with his artificial limb held in place by a large canvas and leather strap buckled over his shoulder. His stump was laced inside a leather corset to hold it in place, and when it was hot in the summer, the stump would often swell and be rubbed raw. My mother helped him to bathe the blisters then cover the stump with fine gauze, so he could go to work. It was impossible to keep him in bed resting, and my mother gave up trying.

Once, when he was ill with more than a touch of bronchitis, the doctor ordered him to stay in bed for a few days to have a rest, but my father decided he knew better than the doctor, and had every intention of getting up and going out to meet his friends for a drink at his local pub. My mother, in desperation, had hidden his artificial leg and after a very noisy argument during which, to my horror – I was listening at the bottom of the stairs – he threatened to jump down the stairs and hop out without it. She gave up and returned the leg. The next day, he was back at work.

Six months after my mother's death in 1982, my father had a very mild stroke; he fell in the road and suffered a hairline fracture of his skull. We thought at first he had been knocked down by a car, but this was not so. The poor motorist who'd nearly hit him as he fell was very distressed. Fortunately, he managed to stop just in time. Surprisingly the young doctor on duty in the hospital casualty department that Sunday was my cousin's son, Ian. He was surprised to find that his patient was the Uncle Jim he had often heard his father, my cousin Alec, talk about. My father made a very good recovery from his fall, and after a short spell in hospital he was soon up and about again.

He went into a residential home the following year, where, to his delight, he was one of two men amongst twelve ladies. Most of the ladies vied with each other to attract his attention and flirted with him outrageously. My mother would have been horrified. He whizzed up and down the stairs on the chairlift to his room on the first floor, and occasionally 'escaped' to put a bet on a horse in the local betting shop just around the corner. He was a difficult man to keep down, as he had shown everyone for so many years. He continued to have a few minor strokes for a few years, finally dying peacefully of pneumonia in his ninetieth year.

I am fortunate to have some cine film taken in the summers of the 1960s and '70s at children's birthday parties in my garden, when my sister and her family and my family were all together sitting in the sunshine. My father looks so happy and contented, and also bemused to find himself the centre of this family group.

People who knew both my father and me often said 'You're so like your father'. I can't think of a finer compliment. After his death, when I went to the residential home to collect his belongings, I sat in his room with some very poignant reminders of his life: his artificial limb, propped up in the corner waiting to go back to the Ministry of Pensions; his walking stick; his pipe, finally cold and gone out; and his favourite photograph of him and my mother, sitting in my garden. I have his two medals and his discharge papers issued in 1919.

Chapter Ten

WARTIME EXPERIENCES

When war was declared on 3rd September 1939, there was no surprise or panic, the inevitable had happened. For months, the papers, radio bulletins and Pathé newsreels had been full of pictures and details of the awful events happening in many parts of Europe: the rise of the Nazi Party in Germany, the persecution of the Jews and the massive build-up of the German war machine; and unspeakable atrocities were committed in the name of the 'fatherland' on the peoples of Czechoslovakia and Poland as they were invaded by German troops.

What was surprising after the declaration was the realisation that preparations must have been secretly taking place for some time – so many things were already in place, and we were quickly on a war footing. Within two weeks, we had all been issued with an identity card giving our name, address and a National Identity number. My number was NIGC/136/4 – the number four meant that I was the fourth member of the household – and I still have the card. Ration books were ready to be issued as soon as the right moment came.

The words and phrases 'appeasement' and 'peace in our time' were often heard from our politicians' lips, but as children

131

we had no idea what they meant. The Prime Minister at the time, Neville Chamberlain, was not a well man and, in the circumstances, proved to be totally inadequate for the job.

In the weeks before war was declared, newsreels were shown of forlorn, bewildered children in London, many in tears, assembling on railway stations about to be evacuated from the capital to safer parts of the country. They waited, with their name tags pinned to their coats, holding a small bag, a suitcase or, sometimes, only a brown paper bag, containing the few possessions they were allowed to take. Round each of their necks hung a small cardboard box containing a gas mask. For some children it was a good experience as they saw the countryside for the first time and they were lucky with their lodgings, but for many children it proved to be a dreadful mistake and they later went back home.

My mother, like many parents, would not let my sister and I be evacuated, we were to stay put and take our chances. She decided that she was the best one to take care of us and, if we were to die, it would be best if we all died together.

My husband had been one of those children standing on a platform in London, waiting for a train to take him away. He was very unhappy with the family he was sent to at first and he didn't stay very long. As soon as he had collected his money from the vicar for singing in the church choir, he took a train back to London and was found by a policeman in a telephone box trying to ring his father. His father was in the army in France, and his mother had died when he was little, so he was taken to stay with his grandmother.

Just as my own father had been affected in the First World War, so too would my husband's father be affected in the Second World

War. At thirty-eight, he was really too old to be on active service. He had joined the regular army in 1919, then after completing his service he joined the Territorial Reserves. When the war started, he found himself in the first wave of troops sent to France, where, as a sergeant, he became a despatch rider, carrying messages between troop positions. This was a dangerous job, as they had to ride at night without lights, they were a target for German snipers, and many were killed. He was evacuated from France via the beaches of Dunkirk, where he stood up to his waist in the water for three days before he managed to get onto a small boat for England. For the rest of his life he suffered from severe bronchitis, finally dying from bronchial pneumonia in 1967.

Gas masks were issued to everyone, with different sizes for adults and children. The white adjustable cotton strap on the canvas cover made it easy to carry the cardboard box over the shoulder. The only problem was, if it rained the box got wet and fell to bits, so those who could afford to, bought covers or had them made from either canvas or leatherette. There was quite a snobbish attitude to the style of cover. The fear of gassing had lingered on in people's minds from the First World War. The horrific scenes of men dying on the battlefields of Flanders, suffering from the effects of the mustard gas used by the Germans, had not been forgotten.

We took our gas masks to school each day, along with our pencil cases and anything else we needed for our lessons. The first gas mask drill was quite difficult to do. The masks were made of strong, black, pungent-smelling rubber, with a metal container underneath holding chemicals and a filter to keep out the gas. They had a large transparent piece of plastic for an eyepiece and a rubber adjustable strap, which went round the back of the head to draw the mask tightly in and ensure a good seal round our faces. When the plastic eyepiece steamed up we could clear it by pressing it close to our faces, the mist would clear and we could see out again. It was a rather frightening and upsetting experience, and some children became quite tearful; they panicked as the smell of the rubber, the chemicals and the claustrophobic feeling of the mask became almost too much for them to bear. After a while, when we realised we were not going to suffocate or be sick, we turned it into a game. Because of the shape of the masks we pretended to be small piglets with black snouts grunting at each other.

Air-raid drills took place when the sirens sounded, and we learnt to differentiate between the rise and fall of the wailing sound of the warning at the start of an air raid and the long single note of the 'all clear'. Later in the war, we learnt to tell the difference between the engines of the German bombers and 'one of ours'. After the raids ended, the long continuous sound of the 'all clear' was greeted with welcome sighs of relief that we hadn't been hit. We left the air-raid shelters, or wherever we'd gone for safety, and went back to our beds, even if it was only for a few hours. Life had to go on, children had to go to school the next day and adults had to go to work.

Each street appointed an Air Raid Warden to monitor the blackout arrangements for every house. As soon as it grew dark, the warden walked up and down, checking to make sure there wasn't the faintest chink of light showing from any of our windows and doors. All curtains had to be heavy enough and dark enough to stop any light from shining through, and if there was the tiniest bit of light showing, the warden would knock on the door and shout 'Lights!' Street lights were extinguished, so we had to use torches to find our way around, and cigarettes could not be smoked outside.

All households were issued with large reels of sticky brown paper, about two inches wide, to stick on the windows, so that if a bomb landed nearby the paper would hold the glass in place and protect us from flying shards of broken glass. It was amazing the different patterns that could be made from the tape – squares, diamonds and triangles – and some of the patterns on the windows became almost works of art. An unspoken element of competition developed, as neighbours tried to out-do each other to create their own original, individual designs.

Nothing seemed to happen for a while after the issuing of identity cards and ration books, and there was a great feeling of waiting – the so-called 'Phoney War'. The mobilisation of men for the Army, Navy and Air Force proceeded at a steady pace, and people began to stock up gradually on non-perishable foodstuffs. There was no panic; we were still foolish enough to think maybe it would all be over by Christmas.

In 1940, Winston Churchill replaced Chamberlain as Prime Minister. An experienced politician, Churchill had at one time been a Minister of War and he proved to be the right man for the job. His rousing oratory was inspiring; his speeches, which have now entered the history books, gave everyone the will to believe that we would eventually win through.

The daily dog fights over South East England, mainly Kent, between our Spitfires and Hurricanes and the German Messerschmit fighters protecting their Heinkel bombers during September 1940 were heard on the radio and watched with horror, not only by people on the ground, but on newsreels at the cinema. Hundreds of young pilots were killed, and survivors were often very badly burned, becoming 'guinea pigs' for Archibald McIndoe and his team of plastic surgeons.

Many goods started to disappear from the shops as rationing began to really take hold. Tea, sugar, butter, meat, bacon and coal were rationed; oranges and bananas were no longer available, and, because of the sugar shortage, each person was only allowed two ounces of sweets a week, four ounces of meat or sausages per person and one bag of coal per household. Clothing coupons were introduced for shoes and clothes, making it very difficult to buy new things. Only when you had saved enough coupons could you go out and buy what was available. I remember in order to purchase a new pair of knickers you needed three coupons. For anyone with a special occasion, such as a wedding, it was very difficult, and family members would often help out by offering a few of their precious coupons, which they had carefully saved for many months.

My mother spent a lot of her time standing in queues. Word would get around quickly when a food delivery arrived in a shop, and a queue would form fast. Due to the lack of oranges and other sources of vitamin C, the small bottles of concentrated orange juice sent over from America were given only to children and pregnant women. Pregnant women were given priority in the shops and ushered to the front of the queues.

Rabbits were not part of the meat ration; it only applied to beef, pork and lamb. The butchers sold rabbits and hares, and fishmongers also sold rabbits to supplement their supplies of fish, which had dwindled because many of the fishermen had been called up and the U-boats posed a danger to the trawlers. The rabbits were bought skinned and ready to cook. My mother would make rabbit and potato pie with some herbs, onions and a thick, crumbly pastry crust, held up by a white china pie funnel – it was a good hearty meal. Now, though, I couldn't bring myself to eat a rabbit.

Billeting officers were appointed to find rooms for men and sometimes women who had to be moved around the country, in order to work in the factories producing essential goods for the war effort. Billeting officers had the power to inspect your home, count the number of rooms, the number of occupants and decide whether or not you had a spare room available. If you didn't take in a lodger, you had to do war work. People had to work wherever they were directed, there was no choice.

Munitions, aero engines, tanks, guns and shipbuilding were priority industries, and engineers with skills in these areas were very much in demand. Many skilled engineers were given exemption from the services, and women who were able to would work in order to release men for the Armed Forces. Once again, as in the First World War, women took over many of the jobs formerly done by men. Not only did they do most of the civilian jobs, such as clerical duties, but they were conscripted into the armed forces to take over the non-combat duties to free the men for the front line.

My cousin Betty had to leave her typing job in an office and go to work in a factory producing aircraft parts. Whilst she had been working in her office, she'd been having her voice trained; she had hoped to have a career singing on the stage. She thought the war had put an end to all her dreams, but she was wrong. Fate took over and the BBC ran a radio programme called Workers' Playtime, a light entertainment show broadcast every day at lunchtime from a factory canteen 'somewhere in Britain'. Betty was lucky. After an audition she was picked as a representative of her factory and she sang on some of the BBC programmes. Her beautiful voice was heard over the radio by many people, and from then on she was billed as Britain's answer to Deanna Durbin, the Hollywood actress who sang and danced in sentimental love stories.

Betty eventually went to London and joined the famous impresario Emile Littler's theatre company, singing in productions of *The Quaker Girl* and *The Song of Norway*. Betty thought that working in a factory was going to be a disaster and would end her dream of a singing career, but it turned into her lucky break. The war had given her the career she had dreamed of and opportunities she may never have had.

In the summer of 1947, when The Song of Norway came to the Empire Theatre in Liverpool, we went to hear Betty sing. She did not appear on stage, as she was the sound echo for the lead. Betty and a couple of cast members stayed with Auntie Elsie and the rest of the cast stayed in 'theatrical digs'. Sunday was their day off, so a party was arranged and most of the cast and the family went on a daytrip to the beach at Hoylake, on the Wirral. I was fifteen at the time and so excited and thrilled to be with this amazing group of people – it was certainly a day to remember!

In London, just after the war, Betty met and married her husband, Syd, a ballet dancer who had worked as a frogman in the Navy during the war, specialising in underwater demolition. He had returned to the stage for a short time, until he could decide what to do in the future.

Betty's mother, my Auntie Elsie, had very strong objections to the wedding because Syd was twelve years older than Betty, and she swore she would not attend the wedding. She changed her mind at the last moment when she realised the wedding was going to go ahead without her. I have a lovely photograph of Betty and Syd at their wedding at Caxton Hall in West London. At that time it was a very fashionable place to be married, favoured by many stars of stage and screen. It was all so romantic. Betty and Syd were embarking on a marriage that was to last for nearly fifty years. Thinking back, it seems to me that Auntie Elsie thought because she was the oldest female member of the family she had the right to dictate what other people should do with their lives – what a good job no one took any notice of her!

Many women who were single and not previously engaged in war work joined the forces. The women's services were: Auxiliary Territorial Service (Army); Women's Auxiliary Air Force (Air Force); Women's Royal Naval Service (Navy), and the Women's Land Army. The girls in the Land Army were there to replace the male farm workers who had gone into the forces. After the war, once they had experienced their freedom, many women never returned to their old jobs.

Men who refused to fight, who declared to be conscientious objectors, were often sent to work in the mines, or made to do other essential work.

Men and women who were too old for active service, or not fit enough, volunteered for the Home Guard, the Auxiliary Fire Service (AFS), the Civil Defence and the Ambulance Service. In the evenings and at weekends, after they had completed their day jobs, they would don their khaki and dark blue uniforms in order to help with the war effort. When the bombing began, the AFS proved to be one of the most dangerous of the voluntary services. A lot of the fire engines were fairly small and unsuitable for fighting so many major fires. At the height of the air raids, there were nights when people stood on a hill in Aughton, about twelve miles to the north of Liverpool, and watched the docks burning.

The sinking of the pride of the navy, the battleship HMS *Hood*, which was blown out of the water, resulting in the loss of 1,400 lives, came as a tremendous shock. Hit in the magazine, the ship never stood a chance. The news stands were covered with black and white pictures of the ship and graphic headlines told the story; it was in all the newspapers and on every radio bulletin. People stood in groups, talking in hushed voices, looking with horror at pictures of the dying ship, their thoughts going out to the relatives of all those who had been killed.

After seeing the humiliating scramble to get our troops off the beaches at Dunkirk as the British Army retreated from France in disarray, and watching the massive flotilla of small boats which bravely crossed the Channel in appalling conditions to help them, it really began to dawn on people that our backs were against the wall and we were in for a long fight.

German U-boats roamed the Atlantic sinking thousands of tons of shipping. In Liverpool, an underground room below the Exchange Flags was the operational centre for planning the Battle of the Atlantic and is now open to the public. In peacetime, Liverpool had been a busy international port, and there was hardly a family without someone in the Merchant Navy or the Royal Navy. It was not surprising when news began to come in that many of the men that were on ships that had been lost at sea were from the area.

Oil tankers were prime targets, as oil was so essential to the war effort, and the husband of my mother's friend was on an oil tanker which was torpedoed. There was very little hope of survivors from a bombed or torpedoed tanker; the ships turned into fireballs and sank very quickly. Anyone with a relative on a tanker lived in dread of that particular telegram arriving. Battered ships, the survivors of convoys attacked by U-boats, limped into port with battle-weary crews. One of my father's good friends was lost on the merchant cruiser HMS *Rawalpindi*, sunk off the Faroe Islands by the fearsome German battle cruisers the *Scharnhorst* and the *Gneisenau*.

My Uncle Alec who, before the war, had been a joiner, producing fine furniture, was now conscripted into working on ship repair. He worked round the clock, often sleeping in makeshift quarters in damp conditions on board the ships, going home only to change into dry clothes. Ships had to be repaired and put back into service as soon as possible. At the end of the war, because of the damp conditions he had worked in and the stress he'd been under, he found he had developed TB, which was in a fairly advanced state. A Freemason and a member of two lodges, he was offered the chance to go to Switzerland for treatment, the trip to be paid for by his fellow masons, but he wouldn't leave his family and he died at home.

I was to find out many years later that my future brother-in-law, who had joined the Merchant Navy at the age of sixteen, had been torpedoed three times and after the last of these attacks was adrift in an open boat for thirteen days.

Various types of air-raid shelters were provided by the government. For houses with gardens there was an Anderson shelter. This was made of sheets of corrugated galvanised steel bolted together, and basic wooden benches were provided to be used as seats or for sleeping on. A deep hole had to be dug into the ground to put the shelter in, before it was then covered with earth. Once the grass had grown over the top of the shelter it looked just like a giant molehill. In the streets where the houses had no back gardens, brick shelters were built to accommodate about 200 people. There was also an indoor shelter for houses, like a metal cage with two mesh sides, which could be placed under a large table or under the stairs.

One night during the May Blitz of 1941, my father, who was on air-raid duty at the time, watched with horror as he saw the silk parachute of a mine shining brightly in the moonlight, floating silently down, holding its deadly cargo. It was drifting over the school, about a quarter of a mile away. The mine had been aimed at the railway line which ran behind the school and went straight to the docks, to collect vital supplies arriving from America, such as food, munitions and oil. The sound of the German bombers had faded away and we thought we were safe, even though the 'all clear' had not yet sounded. My father dashed into the house and told us to get under the stairs as quickly as we could. Seconds later, there was a deep thud, a loud bang and the earth shook for a couple of seconds. The 'all clear' sounded and we breathed a sigh of relief that we hadn't been hit. It wasn't until early the next morning that we realised the full extent of the dreadful tragedy that had happened just a few hundred yards away.

The clear night had been very windy, making the mine blow slightly off course. It had missed the railway line, floated over the school and gone on to make a direct hit to one of the brick air-raid shelters built in the street next to the school, killing nearly 200 people. The shelter had completely disappeared, leaving nothing but a huge crater and some badly damaged houses. An old man standing at the end of the road, out in the open and probably unable to move quickly with fright, had his head blown off by the blast.

School was closed for a couple of weeks and the roads were cordoned off while the site was cleared, the houses deemed too dangerous to be left were knocked down and what was left of the bodies was removed. Some people who'd had to leave their houses for a while were taken in by kind neighbours and relatives who generously opened up their homes. A supermarket now stands on this site.

Nothing was allowed to interfere with our education. If for a brief moment we thought we wouldn't have to go to school because of this disaster, we were sadly mistaken. With the help and encouragement of the school, a group of mothers, including mine, got together and opened up their sitting rooms, where we had lessons every morning, in very mixed groups, from nine until twelve. I was taught by Miss Evans, who was not one of my regular teachers. She was a very tall lady with black cropped hair, a loud booming voice and more than a hint of a moustache. I was convinced she was either a man dressed up as a woman, or even a German spy.

When we were allowed back into school, part of the site was still roped off and sadly there were some empty desks in the classrooms. During assembly we quietly said prayers for all the people who had died and a service was held in our local church; we then got on with our lives.

A couple of miles away, an ammunition train coming from the docks was hit by a bomb giving children what they thought was a spectacular fireworks display. Some very brave men from the Army Bomb Disposal Unit came and uncoupled the undamaged carriages from the one that was exploding and drove the engine away. Nearby houses were evacuated while they dealt with the problem. Many of the houses had some damage – broken windows, minor cracks in the walls and ceilings – but, fortunately, nothing serious enough to stop the occupants from returning home, which was just as well because there were no spare houses for them to go to. Once the train was moved, the Bomb Disposal Unit went off to carry on with its 'normal work', defusing unexploded bombs.

An area of the park where we'd played and had picnics was now sealed off, and guards with guns were placed around it when it was turned into an Ack-Ack (Anti-Aircraft) battery and a searchlight unit, which would light up the night sky and catch the enemy aircraft in their beams, making it easier for the gunners to see their targets. Large silver barrage balloons arrived, which were anchored to the ground by steel cables. Normally they were kept almost on the ground, but when a raid was expected the cables winched the balloons high into the sky to make it difficult for the German planes to reach their targets, forcing them to make a different approach.

Following a raid, we would search for shell caps in the grass around the Anti-Aircraft battery. The metal shell caps were shaped like dunce's hats and golden in colour, with a number painted on. If we were lucky, we also found shrapnel from German bombs in the grass and the surrounding streets. Shrapnel was a shattered piece of either a bomb or a shell case, and the bigger it was the better. The swopping of stamps and marbles took second place to our bartering of these new treasures.

The tall plant rosebay willowherb, with its bright pink flowers, grew well on the derelict bomb sites, and every time I see one it brings back memories of the Blitz.

During another raid, a mine, aimed at the same railway line, missed its target and landed on Anfield Cemetery about a mile away. Pieces of coffins and odds and ends of bones were found around the area. They were quickly collected up by volunteers and the large crater was filled in; we thought it was so funny and made some rude jokes about finding a bottom in a bucket.

Something good came out of this, at least as far as I was concerned. I knew a boy who had managed to get hold of one of the silk ropes that had been attached to the parachute of the mine. He was prepared to exchange it for two of my shell caps. The rope was a thick plait of dozens of strands of white, pure silk, stained green on the outside. Pure silk is noted for its strength and suppleness and would have easily taken the weight of the mine. I saw this as the most beautiful skipping rope I'd ever had. I sped home with my treasure, in case he changed his mind.

I wasn't sure what my mother would say, so I decided to hide the rope in the coal shed. I took it in and out of the shed and showed it off to my friends for some weeks before my mother noticed what I had. When she found out what it was, she was furious, 'How dare you bring that thing in here!' she shouted. 'Wait 'til your father gets home!' It disappeared and I never saw it again. My father told me off in a very half-hearted manner, then he gave me a gentle slap on the legs with a rolled up newspaper. I think he found it quite funny.

Another local tragedy was the direct hit on the Victorian gentlemen's underground toilet in the middle of the crossroad of Spellow Lane and County Road. The raid came suddenly, late one night just as the public houses were closing. Men and women made a dash for the toilet as it was the nearest place to take cover. The warning siren had only just finished its wail when the bombers were overhead, dropping their deadly cargo. No one knew for sure how many people died down there, or who they all were: there may have been as many as ninety. The site is now in the centre of the traffic lights.

Strange things happened during the war. Some people took the opportunity to 'disappear' during air raids, and rumour had it that not all the bodies found after air raids were the victims of the bombing. The police were pretty hard pressed at the time, so probably some murders went unsolved or not investigated.

◄❖:❖►

Once again, as in the First World War, the Commonwealth countries rallied round to help us, including Australians, Canadians, New Zealanders, South Africans, the Ghurkas from Nepal, West Indians, Indians and so many more. The French and Polish soldiers who had managed to escape joined with our forces to fight – some of the airmen who fought so bravely in the Battle of Britain were Polish.

Charles de Gaulle led the Free French contingent, which was based in Britain. When the French sailors began to arrive, their uniforms were very distinctive, with their white flat hats bearing red pom-poms. For some reason it was considered lucky to touch the collar of a French sailor. We daringly nipped up behind them to do this, much to their surprise.

The Americans sent us help in the form of essential supplies of food, much needed oil and ammunition, and lent us 'Liberty' ships to replace those merchant ships sunk by the U-boats. They held back from actual involvement in the fighting, not wanting to repeat the mistakes of the First World War. John Kennedy, the American Ambassador in London at the time and father of the future president of the United States, John F. Kennedy, was of the opinion that we would not be able to survive, and that it was best for America to stay neutral. How wrong he was to underestimate our determination!

To supplement the four ounces per week of our meat ration, we were introduced to the delights of tins of American Spam, a type of tinned pork. It could be sliced, eaten cold, fried, or battered and turned into fritters. Dried egg also came from America, in tins it looked just like custard powder and was best used as an egg supplement for baking. Mixed with water, an omelette could be made from it, but when it was cooked it had the consistency of soft yellow rubber – tasted like it too!

Not far from where I used to live, a small group of Polish families arrived and were accommodated in Nissen huts, set up in the grounds of a large old house that had once been the home of the Hornby family, famous for manufacturing model trains. The families with their strange sounding names all 'z's, 'w's and 'y's were made very welcome, and many of them stayed on after the war was over.

❖❖❖

Notices from the Ministry of Agriculture appeared in large letters on posters on all the billboards, urging anyone who had a garden to 'DIG FOR VICTORY' and help the war effort. The posters showed a picture of a man in his shirt sleeves wearing a waistcoat and baggy trousers tied with string, standing in a garden surrounded by potatoes and other vegetables. His foot was on his spade pushing it firmly into the ground. Lawns were dug up as people who had never grown any vegetables were prepared to have a go.

We didn't have a back garden, only a yard and a small space in front of the house, so we helped my Uncle Harry, who was a very keen gardener, to dig over his back lawn. Once his pride and joy, the lawn was filled with furrows of potatoes, rows of carrots, onions, cabbages and a few lettuces. In his greenhouse, Uncle Harry reduced the number of his beloved chrysanthemums to a minimum and grew tomatoes and cucumbers, giving any surplus he had to his relatives.

Uncle Harry was always pleased to see his nieces and nephews; he was very fond of children. In the late 1920s his first wife had died giving birth to their first child. The baby was large and had died during a long and difficult labour. His wife developed septicaemia; a caesarean operation would probably have saved them both, but in the 1920s the operation was quite rare. I have her gold pocket watch given to her by her grandmother as a keepsake. Later, Uncle Harry married the woman who had been his housekeeper for many years.

Large posters warned us that 'Careless Talk Costs Lives', and we were not to speak in public places about relatives in the forces and where they were – who knew who might be listening. Signposts were removed from the roads in case the enemy invaded, to make it difficult for them to find their way about. The cast-iron railings in front of our houses and around the parks were taken away to help the war effort. We were to find out much later, after the war, when they were discovered in dumps, lying in heaps, that the railings were never used. After all, who had ever heard of a plane or a tank made of cast iron? It was done to trick us into thinking we had made a contribution to the war effort.

In 1940 and 1941, there was very little good news; things seemed to be going from bad to worse. Although we were not fighting in mainland Europe, we were now fighting half way round the world to defend our overseas territories. In North Africa, troops led by Field Marshal Montgomery were fighting the war in the desert against the Germans, led by Rommel, who was nicknamed the 'Desert Fox'. Pathé newsreels showed films of the fierce battles that were fought at El Alamein and Tobruk.

In December 1941, when the Japanese bombed the American Fleet in Pearl Harbour, the Americans entered the war. Although it was an unspeakable act of treachery on the part of the Japanese, as they had not officially declared war, it meant that the most powerful nation in the world had now entered the conflict. After the initial shock of what had taken place, came the realisation that perhaps this could be the turning point.

In the Far East, Singapore fell to the Japanese, seizing their chance to further their territorial ambitions across the Pacific. Thousands of British troops and civilians were interned in Japanese camps. News came in of the unspeakable atrocities committed against the British prisoners of war, both men and women, and of the cruelty inflicted on the native civilian populations of the countries that the Japanese had invaded in the Pacific.

Unlike the Germans, they paid no heed to the rules of the Geneva Convention, which should have applied to all prisoners of war in their camps. Those who survived and finally came home after the war were in a dreadful state both mentally and physically. So too were the prisoners who were forced to work like slaves for the Japanese in Burma, on the notorious railway.

When the Americans started arriving in this country, many of them were stationed on Aintree racecourse, home of the Grand National. They were welcomed with a great deal of curiosity; hardly anyone had seen an American at close quarters before, our images of Americans had been formed from what we had seen on cinema screens. They all seemed so big and well dressed, their army uniforms were so much smarter than those that our soldiers wore.

The Americans brought all their own food and supplies, and didn't seem to be short of anything. They chewed gum continually, and one question that children constantly asked the American soldiers was 'Got any gum chum?' The Americans were very generous with their sweets and gave so many to the delighted local children, who only had a ration of two ounces per week.

The armed guards standing in pairs at the entrances to the racecourse were the biggest men we'd ever seen, some of them were black – I'd never been so close to a black man before. They wore white helmets with the letters 'MP' painted on in large black letters, and white gaiters and belts. They stood at ease with the butts of their rifles resting on the floor. We used to cycle slowly by, then stop and stare in awe at the huge soldiers – to small ten-year-olds they seemed like giants. Our staring was treated with good humour, mostly they stared into space, but occasionally they would break into a smile and give us a wink. When my mother found out where we went, she was furious. If she ever found out that I continued to hang around the racecourse, she said, I would not sit down for a week and I would be kept in for a month.

When some Italian soldiers were taken prisoner and brought to this country, many were sent up to Burscough in Lancashire to work on the local farms. They were free to come and go. We often saw them in Ormskirk when they were off duty. Dressed in their dark brown battledress uniforms with a large coloured diamond on the back, they were easily recognisable; we knew who they were and didn't consider them a threat. They appeared to be quite happy working on the farms, perhaps some of them had been farmers back home in Italy. They were very pleasant and eager to talk to the local people, making no attempt to escape, probably glad to be out of the war. The Italians had been reluctant partners with Germany in the war. Many of the soldiers married local girls and after the war settled in the UK permanently.

As the war in the Pacific progressed, some of the soldiers and civilians taken prisoner by the Japanese began to be released. One day, in 1944, news came through that a Red Cross troopship was landing at Liverpool, full of prisoners of war returning from some of the Japanese camps. They were to go to Aintree for assessment and initial treatment. The racecourse was now nearly empty, except for a few soldiers looking after the supplies – the Americans had gone to the South Coast to prepare for the D-Day landings.

At dusk on a warm sunny evening, as the convoy of army lorries, all bearing a Red Cross, drove slowly by, those in the open-backed lorries who were able to leant out to grasp the hands of the crowds of people who had come to cheer and welcome them home. Tears streamed down the faces of the emaciated troops and of the people looking on. Soldiers who were ill or badly wounded were in closed lorries. It was a very emotional moment, as we saw the visible proof of their dreadful treatment at the hands of the Japanese.

Later on, when more troops came home, among them was one of my uncles. He had been imprisoned for some years by the Japanese in New Guinea. He was in a sorry state, suffering from jungle sores and malnutrition. He had also contracted beriberi and malaria whilst he was in the camp, there was practically no medical treatment provided and very few medicines were available.

Most of the supplies sent by the Red Cross were kept by the Japanese to treat themselves as their supplies were running out. Despite very good medical care when he returned to this country, my uncle never recovered from his illnesses and died about a year later.

Two memorable events near the end of the war will always stay sharply in my mind. As the Allied troops were advancing well into Germany, the full horror of the concentration camps was revealed. We went to the cinema and watched Richard Dimbleby, who was a war correspondent working for the BBC, trying to describe the scenes at Belsen concentration camp. He was with the British troops who had gone in to liberate the camp. He had difficulty describing the scene through his tears. The images of gaunt, hollow-eyed, walking bags of bones, in tattered striped rags, barely able to stand with their arms pleadingly outstretched, spoke for themselves, and the rotting piles of corpses did not need any words. Prisoners were systematically starved to death; some even ate their own faeces in their desperate attempts to stay alive. It was impossible to believe that a so-called civilised nation could have done this. Would this have been our fate if the Germans had invaded Britain?

It was frightening to watch the newsreels of the dropping of the atom bombs on Japan in August 1945, on the cities of Hiroshima and Nagasaki. The gigantic mushroom clouds filled with fire, climbing miles high into the sky, looked as though they would never stop. The devastation was unbelievable, over 100,000 dead and two cities destroyed. What monstrous thing had been created?

Chapter Eleven

MAKE-DO-AND-MEND

The war began to have a noticeable impact on our lives, as more and more goods disappeared off the shelves. The art of make-do-and-mend took on a new meaning, making us find new ways of saving things, mostly the necessities of life which we had taken for granted. All pieces of soap which had become too small to handle were no longer thrown away, they were saved and placed in a white stone jar. When the jar was half full a little water was added, then the jar was placed in a pan of boiling water and kept heated until all the pieces had melted into a multi-coloured jelly. The next morning a marbled cake of soap was tipped out, left to cool and cut into pieces for further use.

Because of the power cuts, candles were in great demand. My mother saved all the ends of used candles and night lights, discarded the old bits of wick, put the candle remnants in a small tin, melted them gently in a pan of water then inserted a new wick. We re-used them as night lights. Brown paper, which had been wrapped round a parcel, was ironed and kept to re-use; string was never cut, the knots were carefully undone then wound into small balls.

Every night before we went to bed my mother filled the kettle with water, in case the water supply was cut off during the night.

Whatever else happened we would be sure of a nice hot cup of tea in the morning to send us off, either to work or to school.

When leather for the soles of shoes became scarce, my father managed to find two old iron cobbler's lasts, one for children's shoes and one for adults. He bought some composite material called Driped, which temporarily replaced leather, and set about repairing our shoes. When he couldn't get Driped he glued rubber soles onto our shoes, which he had cut perfectly to shape.

Recently, when I moved house, I came across the cobbler's lasts in my garage and I gave them to a small local museum of family history, run by a couple of enthusiasts in an old stone barn at the back of their cottage.

Wooden soled shoes became fashionable (they were not clogs, mind). They had stylish uppers with wooden soles which were hinged across the middle of the sole, to make them easy to walk on. They made a bit of a noise, but they served their purpose. My sister had a pair, with brown suede uppers trimmed with orange leather.

Marzipan was difficult to buy, as the ground almonds came from countries in the Middle East, mainly Jordan. For Christmas cakes and birthday cakes, my mother managed to make some using soya flour and almond essence to replace the almonds; the texture and taste were about the same, so it was almost impossible to tell the difference.

Sugar was rationed because it came from the West Indies, and instead saccharin was used for sweetening tea, which unfortunately left a very nasty taste in the mouth. My father was lucky, he was the only one in the house who took sugar in his tea and he never went short. I'd never taken sugar since I had overheard a conversation one night just before the war, between my father, my Uncle Harry and one of his friends, who was the captain on a ship which went back and forth to the West Indies. They'd come back to the house one night for a cup of tea on their way home from the pub. I had gone to bed, but when I heard voices, I sat on the landing with my head poking through the banisters to listen. Grown-up conversations were so interesting. Uncle Harry's friend refused sugar for his tea because, he said, when he looked into the hold of his ship to check the raw cane sugar which was being shipped over from the West Indies for refining, the sugar cane was moving slightly, the movement was caused by the rats in the hold moving about in the sugar cane. I dashed back to bed, pulled the covers over my head and had nightmares about giant rats nibbling my toes.

The next day I looked quite pale and wan and my mother thought maybe I was sickening for something. If I had told her what the problem was, she would have said, 'Serves you right for listening to other people's conversations.' I noticed around that time she also stopped taking sugar. He may have been just telling a very tall tale, but I couldn't be sure and I wasn't going to take any chances.

My Auntie Liz was about to get rid of a coat which was worn round the cuffs and buttonholes. It was made from fine, lightweight, brown tweed with little orange flecks, and she gave it to my mother who had seen some potential in it. It was just what she was looking for. I was growing fast and needed an outfit for a special occasion. Clothing coupons were needed, even for lengths of material and were very precious. My mother had the coat cleaned, before she slowly took it to pieces. First, she cut off the buttons and put them in her button box for future use, then carefully took out the satin lining and unpicked all the seams before she discarded anything that couldn't be used. The woollen part of the coat was treated in the same way. All the seams were unpicked, the worn parts cut away, then every piece was carefully pressed. Because the coat was slightly faded in parts she decided to 'turn' it. The inside of the material was in good condition and had kept its original colour.

A couple of weeks later, and after many hours of careful cutting and sewing, I was resplendent in a pleated skirt with crossover straps, a matching short sleeved bolero and a skull cap. My mother drew round one of her irons to make the shapes for the skull cap. No one could possibly tell the outfit was made from an old coat. To go with this outfit, I had a new blouse of white voile, with tiny green and orange embroidered dots, made from the best parts of the skirt of an old summer dress.

Knitting wool was scarce, so my father's white stump socks were a godsend! They were made from soft, pale cream-coloured wool and arrived every three months by post from the Ministry of Pensions. They were tubular shaped, like a long finger-stall, and were all the same length so they could be cut to size, according to the length of the stump – my father's socks were about eight inches too long. Once the ends had been very carefully cut off, we set about unravelling the wool and wound it into balls. It was a bit crinkly, but when the finished articles were pressed with a damp cloth and a hot iron they soon flattened out. We knitted jumpers, cardigans, bed socks, a woolly tea cosy and some dolls' clothes, and pot holders made from odd scraps of cloth left over from dressmaking were stuffed with bits of the wool. As far as I was concerned, the best things we knitted were Sonja Henie hats and mittens.

Sonja Henie was a star in American films. She had come originally from Czechoslovakia, where she had shot to fame by winning the Ladies' World Figure Skating Championship and an Olympic Gold medal. She was blonde, petite, pretty, and was soon snapped up by Hollywood. She looked like a fairy princess as she sped over the ice, performing spectacular jumps, and spinning so fast that it was difficult to count the number of spins. Her golden hair gleamed, her sequinned dresses sparkled and her silver skates flashed in the spotlights.

A knitting pattern came out showing a pretty young woman wearing Sonja Henie's hat and mittens. We wanted to look like her, and so all we had to do was buy the pattern and knit the hat and mittens. These were knitted with the white wool that we'd so carefully unpicked from the stump socks. Along the front of the hat was a padded patterned band about three inches wide. The pattern was of five large snowflakes knitted in red and made to look like flowers with a yellow spot in the middle surrounded by some small green leaves. Each snowflake was separated by a band of blue. The hat tied under the chin with strands of coloured wool, twisted together, ending in multi-coloured pom-poms. The backs of the mittens were quartered, and each quarter contained a red snowflake separated by a thin blue band. We knitted them not only for ourselves but as Christmas presents for our cousins.

Before I can describe the blue crêpe and the wartime sewing session, I will have to tell you more about my mother's sisters. Elsie, the eldest, always considered herself to be in charge. Lizzie came next. She was very different from the other four – Lizzie could hold her drink, smoked like a chimney and was divorced. In the 1940s divorce was quite rare. She managed a butcher's shop, and in her spare time in the evenings, she served behind the bar in a pub called The Prince Albert, and she liked to be in male company. Alice, my mother, the one in the middle of the five, was a quiet hazel-eyed person with light brown hair, who always appeared to be a little on the outside of the circle. Auntie Margaret was next, and she worked in a hairdresser's. In her spare time she produced beautiful hand-knitted garments for anyone who asked. While she knitted at speed, she chain-smoked. Emma was the youngest. Emma married suddenly in her mid-thirties in a registry office during the war, to a French-Canadian pilot named Phillipe. This turned out to be a disaster and became quite a family scandal. I am still not sure of the details, as a policy of 'not in front of the children' was strictly applied. Soon after her marriage, Emma found she was pregnant and Phillipe suddenly had a posting overseas. When Emma visited his commanding officer to claim her wife's allowance, the storm broke. Phillipe already had a wife back home in Canada! Floods of tears and very heated discussions took place behind closed doors. We children (all the cousins) tried desperately hard to find out what was going on. Any inquiry was met with stony-faced silence and a stern warning to 'Mind your own business'. The words 'bigamy' and 'solicitor' were heard as we eavesdropped on one of the conversations. We had to look bigamy up in the dictionary as we were not really sure what it meant, but we soon found out. My father recommended a good solicitor, who had done some business for a friend. We never saw Phillipe again.

I have to admit, at the time I didn't know what all the fuss was about. I had a soft spot for my Uncle Phillipe. On one of his trips back to Canada he'd brought a very exciting present back for me

– a beautiful pair of ice-skates with white leather boots. I dreamt
of becoming the next Sonja Henie.

In the ensuing family crisis, Margaret, or Meg as she liked to be
called, proved to be a tower of strength. She lived quite a distance
away and took Emma to live in her house as a 'war widow'. Meg
promptly set to work, knitting like fury with one needle tucked
firmly under her armpit, chain-smoking as she turned out masses
of baby clothes with the speed of a knitting machine.

I had to explain all this because Phillipe, who was working
ferrying bombers over from Canada, provided the means that
was to keep the women in the family busy for a few months –
twenty-nine yards of pale-blue lingerie crêpe, sprinkled with
pale pink roses. Clothing for most of the war years was difficult
to buy. The crêpe had been smuggled in from Canada so we
were not to tell anyone about it, or boast that we were about to
have some new garments, which added to the excitement.

Fortunately, all the sisters, except Lizzie, could sew. We were
assembled round Elsie's large dining room table, which had
to have both the leaves opened out to give plenty of space to
spread the material on. My aunts, my sister, Joyce, my cousins,
Dorothy, Margaret, Betty, and me all had our measurements
taken to make sure every available scrap of the precious
material was put to good use. Sizes of busts, waists, shoulder
to waist, shoulder to knee and shoulder to elbow were all duly
noted. Cutting so many items from the one piece of material
meant that every available scrap could be used.

My Auntie Elsie's best friend Dolly was brought in to help, who
was now engaged on very important war work – the cutting and
sewing of parachutes. Before the war, Dolly had been a tailoress
but she'd had to choose between taking a lodger into her

immaculate house or do war work. She chose the parachutes. Every precious scrap of the off-cuts and pieces of white pure silk that were left over from the making of parachutes was put to good use. Many a wartime bride walked down the aisle in a wedding dress made from them.

There were only three good patterns, and as we were all different shapes and sizes they had to be either split and newspaper inserted to make them larger, or folded with a pleat to make them smaller, according to who the item was for.

Weeks of work sewing and stitching the blue crêpe eventually provided every female member of the family with a blouse of exactly the same shape and style, buttoned up the front with puff sleeves, and a plain yoke, with the bodice material gathered onto it, a camisole and one petticoat. The petticoats were finished round the hems with hand-sewn shell stitching, and again they were all the same style. We were still wearing some of the blouses and slips after the war had ended, and we remarked that if we had all fallen over together, there would have been acres of blue crêpe to see. The mere mention of the blue crêpe was enough to make us smile.

Of my mother's sisters, Lizzie died first, aged fifty-eight, of a disease called 'dropsy'. Meg, aged sixty-four, had two massive heart attacks. My mother, Alice, born in the middle, died of leukaemia a few weeks short of her eightieth birthday. Emma finally moved in with Elsie and they lived together for over forty years; both died in 1988 within a few days of each other. Elsie, who was nearly ninety-four and had suffered with arthritis for some time, was found to have developed cancer, and Emma who was eighty-four and had been caring for Elsie, went to bed the next day and two days later died in her sleep.

On the day of Elsie and Emma's funeral, the rest of the family was assembled round the large oak table in Elsie's house. The table was opened out fully and laid with the best damask tablecloth, which it only was for christenings, weddings, funerals and Christmas. Those of us who were there during the war, when the blue crêpe was cut and sewn, suddenly started to laugh and cry at the same time, remembering the tissue patterns, newspaper gussets, flashing scissors, tape measures and small bodies standing shivering in their Liberty bodices, waiting to be fitted for blouses and slips. We were amazed to find that in what appeared to be a twinkling of an eye, we had become the old aunts and uncles.

In America in 1938, nylon thread had been made into a commercially viable product. It was spun by the DuPont company into stockings, and was a complete revolution in the making of ladies' stockings; all our hosiery until then was made from either pure silk or fine lisle. Stockings always had a seam right down the middle of the leg at the back, with a small thicker area coming partly up the back of the heel. It was so important to make sure the seams were straight, the last thing women did before they left the house was to check their seams. Nylon stockings had only just begun to appear in the shops when the war came. Because they were in such short supply, word flew round quickly if a shop took delivery of some nylons and only one pair per customer was allowed. They were sold in shoe sizes, and women were prepared to pay £1 per pair! They were so precious they were kept in glass jam jars when they were not being worn, why I am not quite sure – probably to prevent snagging.

A ladder in a stocking was a catastrophe, and a new service sprang up in dry cleaning shops which offered a repair service.

In the window of the shop a woman who did invisible darning on items of clothing, operated a small electric machine which re-knitted each ladder with a tiny hook. The charge for the repair was made according to the number of stitches that had been dropped.

I stood in front of the window and watched the machine whiz up the ladder with the stitch. I realised that if I had one of the tiny hooks which were on sale I could do my own repairs. After a shaky start I became pretty good at hooking the tiny stitches back up over each one of the threads. Not only did I painstakingly repair my own stockings but I did those of my sister, my mother and a few special friends. The one thing it really needed was patience and a good smooth clear-glass tumbler to stretch the stocking over. Nylon stockings and tights are no longer repaired in this way, once they are laddered they are thrown away.

❖❖❖

Hobbies and things to do produced some quite ingenious things. One that was very unusual was the brooches we made from the bones in a cod's head. When my mother managed to buy a whole cod she would steam it then cut off the head. Before the head was thrown away she would remove the flesh, then wash, dry and keep the bones. Once the white bones were cleaned and dried, we set about making brooches by decorating the bones using tiny pots of Humbrol paints. The brooches were very bright and shiny and looked like abstract paintings. After the paint had dried we applied jeweller's glue on the back to hold a small gilt safety pin.

To make bracelets we wove multi-coloured lengths of thin electrical wire together, mainly red, green, blue and black.

Brooches were also made from scraps of leather cut into heart shapes, boots, rabbits, dogs and cats, then stuffed with kapok and fitted with a small safety pin, sometimes tiny beads or sequins were sewn on to make them more decorative. If we could find a bit of lace, that too was sewn on as a frill.

Something else we did, was to make brooches by winding fine copper electrical wire round a very thin knitting needle, to make what looked like a spring, it was twisted round to form the shape of either a flower petal or a butterfly's wing, depending on what type of brooch we were making. Silko sewing cotton of various colours was then threaded carefully round the wire. The brooches trembled and quivered gently when worn and it looked as though the butterfly was really flying. Idle hands made mischief we were told, so we were kept very busy.

Undamaged milk bottle tops were washed and kept, then used to make woollen pom-poms to decorate our winter hats and mittens. We made pom-poms by putting two of the tops together, then, with a bodkin – a large blunt-ended needle with an eye big enough to take wool – we threaded coloured lengths of wool through the hole in the centre and round the discs, until the hole was so full that we couldn't thread any more wool through. With a small pair of scissors we would carefully insert a blade through the wool between the tops and cut through. Once the wool was cut, and while the two discs were still in place, a length of wool was bound tightly round the centre. We would then pull the cardboard tops out and – hey presto! – the wool sprang open and became a pom-pom.

Nothing was wasted: when chamois leathers became difficult to buy, my mother resorted to using a good old-fashioned remedy to clean her windows – a newspaper dipped in water containing a teaspoon of vinegar. Bicarbonate of soda replaced toothpaste for a little while, as this was not only good as a disinfectant but it helped to keep our teeth white.

When I was eight, I joined a troop of dancers who did tap and ballet, called the Co-op Sunbeams, because we rented the Co-op Hall every Saturday morning for two hours. It was a tram ride away so my mother would take me, do some shopping, then call back for me later. Once I had mastered the intricacies of the first, second, third and fourth time-steps and the American Roll I thought I was a star. I was given a pair of red leather shoes with toe and heel taps. The metal taps made scratches on the quarry tiles of the kitchen floor when I practised my routines, so my father managed to get hold of an old drawing board for me to dance on. Mercifully, it deadened the noise of the constant rhythm of tap, tap, tap, tap, tap …

The difficulty we had, or rather our mothers had, was trying to find material to make the costumes for our concerts. At the beginning of 1943, all the local dancing groups were to combine, to present a grand concert in St George's Hall, which was to be performed before hundreds of troops who were on embarkation leave prior to being shipped abroad to fight. St George's Hall is a famous neo-classical building in a commanding position right in the centre of Liverpool. It was used for very special occasions, such as the quarterly assizes. During the war, its beautiful mosaic floor was covered over with wooden planks to save it from damage. Our group was to perform three of our best numbers: the Cowgirls sequence, April Showers and Waltzing in the Clouds. Because there were so many children taking part, we had to change into our costumes in the Walker Art Gallery then run across the road to St George's Hall.

The Cowgirls sequence was performed to the tune of 'Idaho' by Eddy Arnold. It was quite amazing, someone always knew someone who had just the thing we were looking for. We asked no questions and from an unnamed warehouse came some fine black, cotton-backed oiled cloth, which looked like leather. It was used in factories, what for I am not sure, but it served our purpose. This would be fine for the skirts, boleros and hats for the cowgirls. The bottom of the skirts and the edges of the boleros were carefully cut into strips, to resemble fringes. The hats were just a large brim with straps across the crown. The blouses to go with this outfit were made from very coarse purple net that scratched our skins, particularly under the arms.

From the same source we also managed to get hold of some bright red, very shiny oilcloth, normally used for tablecloths, to make the outfits for the raindrops number. We had short flared skirts and large bows to put on our heads. This number was danced to the tune of 'Drip Drip Drop Little April Showers'. As we danced in the outfits we grew very hot and there was a strong smell of oil.

The material for the dresses for the Waltzing in the Clouds number proved a little more difficult. Finally, in an army supply depot some old surplus mosquito netting was unearthed. Washed, bleached, starched, then fashioned into long floaty dresses with frills round the bottom and up the front, who could tell what they were made from? This number was our finale and was danced to a Deanna Durbin song, 'Waltzing in the Clouds'.

We went home thrilled, exhausted and happy to have performed on such a magnificent stage in such a beautiful building. I shudder to think what the troops thought of it, they were probably glad to get away!

⟨❖:❖⟩

A black market sprang up, nearly always in the back rooms of pubs, where bacon, pork joints, kidneys, pigs trotters or even a pig's head to make brawn could be bought at a price from someone who had reared a pig and not declared it to the authorities. The occasional chicken and tins of Cucumber brand Alaskan salmon often found their way onto our dinner tables.

From large suitcases on street corners, away from watchful eyes, men sold pairs of nylon stockings, cheap watches, hair clips, combs and lots of other items too numerous to mention. They disappeared with their suitcases with remarkable speed when a policeman appeared. Buying some of these things could often be a big mistake, especially with the nylons, when you opened the packet, you could find that one stocking was longer than the other, or the feet were not the same size. That was a risk you had to be prepared to take. The watches lasted a very short time before stopping.

My ability to make-do-and-mend has stayed with me. My son has often had to remind me, 'The Germans have surrendered, the war is over.' Not for me it isn't!

Chapter Twelve

THE LIGHTS COME ON AGAIN

Just after the troop concert in 1943, I had to give up tap dancing to concentrate on other things. At school I was in the scholarship class, and I'd passed the first stage, the Review, and the scholarship exam was to take place in a few weeks. My parents had promised me a new bicycle if I passed the exam. I was desperately in need of one. For a couple of years I'd put up with an old second-hand bike that my father had managed to buy from one of his sisters for just £2.

It was in a very poor state, all the chromium parts were rusty and the paint was flaking off, but with a lot of emery paper and hard work I managed to make it look a lot better. I repainted it every couple of weeks to keep it looking shiny, but the paint never seemed to set hard and it always felt sticky, and quite often some of it came off on my legs. What I hated most about the bike was the style; it was a 'sit up and beg' one, just like the one that Nurse Roan had ridden, but much older.

I had my heart set on a bike with cable brakes, Sturmey-Archer three-speed gears and lots of chromium which would sparkle in the sunshine. During the first few years of the war very few new bikes had been made, and those that were

168

made were all black, as chromium was needed for hardening steel and for other uses in the war effort. Some were now slowly beginning to come back onto the market, made by a firm called British Small Arms (BSA), whose logo was three crossed rifles.

I stood outside the window of a cycle shop called Jack Styles, in Liverpool, and picked out my model. All that was needed was for me to pass the exam and it would be mine. As I worked my way steadily through the book of Arithmetic and English questions which had been given to those who were to sit the exam, providing examples of what we might expect, I kept the picture of the bicycle firmly in my mind. I still have the book, and I'm quite sure that most of today's sixteen-year-olds would have difficulty answering the questions.

We had received a card from the Education Committee giving instructions for the exam, which was to take place in Holly Lodge High School at 9.30 a.m. on 5th March 1943. I was to take with me the card which bore my candidate number, two pens (in case a nib broke), two pencils, an India rubber and a ruler. Paper was to be provided, with arrival to be strictly before 9.10 a.m.

I was up early; I dressed in my best turquoise blue coat and petrol blue beret with an orange and brown feather. As I walked into the exam room, holding my candidate's card and my writing equipment firmly in my hands, I was determined the bike would be mine.

A couple of months later, when the results came through, I was so excited to learn I had passed the exam, and later in the year, in September, I would be starting at Queen Mary High School. I went to Jack Styles with my father to collect my bike, it had been taken out of the window because my mother had been in and put down a deposit on it of 10/-. I wheeled it home because I was not sure how to use the three speed. I soon found out that it wasn't so difficult.

For passing the scholarship, my Uncle Harry gave me a £5 note, one of the large white thin paper ones with all the lettering and curly decorations in black. I had never held so much money of my own in my hand!

The next thing was a visit to the school outfitters to be measured for my blazer and buy the velour hat, hatband and school tie. Instructions were sent from the school about other items of uniform I would need and where to buy the name tapes to sew on all my school clothes. At a meeting in the school hall we bought text books and hockey sticks off the girls who were leaving, which was a very good idea as my parents had to pay for my books. My mother was also given a leaflet showing a diagram of the type of gym tunic I would have to wear for games – light blue cotton for summer and another in navy blue wool for winter. The style was very simple and easy to make.

Once again, September was to bring another major change in my life. I was off to struggle with Latin verbs, the joys of the French language, Algebra, Geometry and Science. I would no longer skip to school; I could go on my new bike. Each morning before I left the house, my mother would stand at the door and check to make sure I had my homework, my dinner ticket, my pencil case and most importantly a clean handkerchief.

At Christmas in 1943, at the end of the first term in my new school, anyone who could knit and follow a basic pattern was given some skeins of khaki knitting wool and a leaflet containing simple instructions, all supplied by the Red Cross. We were going to knit mittens, gloves and Balaclava hats for the Russian troops, who in the grip of a freezing cold Russian winter were fighting fierce battles against the Germans and were very short of supplies of basic items of equipment.

Over the Christmas holidays, after winding the skeins of wool into balls, I knitted steadily, working my way through the patterns. I was so pleased to be making such a contribution to the war effort and I tried to picture the Russian soldiers who would be kept warm, wearing the things I had knitted.

The year 1943 was proving to be a turning point in the war. It was far from over, but we slowly began to realise that we were eventually going to win. The air raids had stopped some time ago and our gas masks were stored away in cupboards. The stirrup pump and the rest of the fire fighting equipment were stowed away in the coal shed, just in case we might need them again.

When Vera Lynn, the forces sweetheart, sang 'The White Cliffs of Dover' and 'When the Lights Go on Again', all over the world we believed her. The Americans, with their huge war machine now fully geared up, were slowly fighting their way back across the Pacific, island by island, in some of the fiercest and bloodiest battles of the war.

Squadrons of American planes, huge bombers known as flying fortresses, and fighters were based in airfields in East Anglia, operating with the RAF, concentrating on strategic targets in Germany. So many young men lost their lives. Shipping losses, however, had decreased because the U-boats no longer controlled the Atlantic.

For a time, another threat was to hit these islands. The Germans had been building sites on the Dutch coast to launch their V2 rockets, which were aimed at London and the South

East. The engines of these huge unmanned rockets suddenly cut out and the rockets plunged to earth. People just grew to live with them for a while. They stopped when they heard them, waited until the rocket engine had cut out, listened for the bang, then they got on with their work. The rockets had been developed by the German scientist Dr Werner von Braun, who, at the end of the war, was whisked off to America to help in the development of rockets for the American space programme. He was taken to America to stop the Russians capturing him for their rocket programme.

D-Day, 6th June 1944, was the day we had waited for, for nearly five years. The Allied troops landed in France, and after some very fierce fighting had established a beach-head. But the war in Europe was far from over. It was to be another year before the German military command finally surrendered, and the Japanese were still fighting hard in the Pacific, refusing to surrender. The dropping of atom bombs on Japanese cities by the Americans in August 1945, brought about a quicker end to the war in the East.

In the winter of 1944, in the Ardennes in Belgium, at Bastogne the 101st Airborne Division fought a fierce battle with the Germans for control of a major crossroads and tens of thousands American troops were killed. This battle was to become known as the Battle of the Bulge. I mention this battle, because many years later, in 1962, driving through Belgium on our way to Switzerland, my husband and I went through the Ardennes and stopped at Bastogne, a quiet little town at the edge of the Ardennes forest. At the corner of the square was an American tank with its gun pointing right down the hill of one of the main approach roads. White stars on its sides and the words

101st Airborne Division proclaimed it to be one of the tanks that had fought in the battle. As we walked slowly round the square, experiencing our first packet of chips topped with mayonnaise, I found it hard to accept that this was the place where the battle had played out. We went into the museum in the square and saw photographs of the appalling devastation which had been inflicted on the lovely old town. Amazingly, all the buildings had been lovingly rebuilt using old photographs and plans, and such care had been taken to restore the area to its original state. To heal the scars on the landscape was probably the best way to pay tribute to the many thousands of lives that had been lost trying to gain control of this piece of land.

In 1945, when peace was declared, all round the country church bells which had been silenced during the war rang out to celebrate victory. Street parties were organised and bonfires lit, which many people used as a means of getting rid of old unwanted pieces of furniture – so many old pianos were burnt on bonfires in the celebrations. Flags and bunting were brought out and stretched across the streets. Although it was hard to believe, after nearly six years of war, the lights really had come on again, and so had the neon signs in Piccadilly in London.

The climax of the celebrations was the huge Victory Parade held in London, before King George VI, Queen Elizabeth, Princess Elizabeth and Princess Margaret. Princess Elizabeth wore her army uniform. During the war she had trained as a driver in the ATS.

There was a feeling of hope and expectancy in the air. Brothers and fathers were very slowly beginning to come home from their units. But rationing was still in place and would be for a few more years, ending in the 1950s, and we still had many difficulties to cope with and problems to solve, not least the housing shortage which would take some time to solve.

Many marriages were in trouble because of the long periods of separation, and due to the difficulty of adjusting to changed circumstances some did not survive. Women who'd had relationships and children with Americans, who'd promised to take them back to America after the war, found out this was not going to happen. Troops serving abroad for a long time had also found new partners.

On the whole our family came out of the war almost unscathed. Our houses had suffered very little damage, just some broken windows from bomb blasts, and the damage to Auntie Margaret's house from the undercarriage of a train going through the roof of her back bedroom, was soon repaired. The one casualty was my uncle, who died soon after he came home from the Japanese prison camp. Compared with what some people had suffered, this was quite bearable.

We had coped with the rationing and shortages and we never really went without any of the essentials. Due to my mother's ingenuity and hard work she was able to give us good meals, with plain but well-cooked food. We were careful with our clothing coupons and in addition to our efforts at make-do-and-mend, we managed to buy what we needed to dress reasonably well.

Families, friends, neighbours and even passing strangers came together to help and support each other willingly when necessary.

Chapter Thirteen

CYCLING TO SCHOOL

September 1945 – the start of the autumn term. This was the first school year to begin in peace time for six years. To me it really felt like a new beginning, as I cycled happily along on my bike down the tree-lined dual carriageway, I passed Walton Hall Park, where I had collected newts as a child and where the Ack-Ack gun battery and the barrage balloons had been installed during the war. I was now thirteen-and-a-half and I felt quite grown up. I was looking forward to seeing all my school friends again. Drama and music played quite a part in our curriculum, and each year the school put on a major production, either a play or one of Gilbert and Sullivan's operettas. As I cycled, I wondered what it would be this year.

During the holidays I'd had my hair cut. I no longer had plaits and I wore my hair tied back in two bunches of curls held in place by navy blue ribbons. My mother had even agreed to let me have a very soft perm on the ends of my hair to make it a little curlier.

I usually cycled to school with my friend Mary. She was never ready when I called for her and would rush to get dressed and finish her breakfast while I sat outside on my bike waiting for her.

Mary seemed to be accident prone: one morning when I called for her, she dashed out of bed so quickly she broke her big toe by stubbing it on the end of the bed. In school she fell off the vaulting horse in the gym, dislocating her shoulder and giving herself a marvellous black eye.

One sunny day in 1944, Mary and I were cycling to school, talking about our plans for the next holiday, when Mary was accidently knocked off her bike by an American Jeep. It was only a gentle push but her collarbone was dislocated and she suffered severe bruising, and she had to stay in hospital for a week. The Americans were very upset and Mary was showered with gifts of chocolates, sweets, chewing gum and, best of all, a pair of white buckskin shoes with blue check laces. I was consumed with envy. I would have been prepared to have a dislocated collarbone and a short stay in hospital if it meant I could have had all those goodies. Why couldn't it have been me? I had to take schoolwork home to Mary and collect what she had done, to make sure she kept up with everything. Illness was no excuse to get out of school work. I was only too pleased to do this, as it meant I could share some of Mary's chocolates and gum. When she left school, Mary went on to dedicate her life to nursing, rising to great heights in the profession; in the circumstances, it was probably the best career for her.

It felt good to be returning to Queen Mary. This autumn term I was starting my third year and I would be moving to the upper fourth, the Senior School. I loved school. I enjoyed learning new things, taking part in activities and being presented with new challenges. I liked the sense of order and the friends I had made, school was a good place to be. Cycling to school that pleasant, warm, September morning, I wondered if any changes had taken place during the summer.

The big talking point amongst us all at the start of the year was Veronica! She had been expelled at the end of the summer term. Veronica was someone in the sixth form who we all admired. Her bright blonde hair shone like a beacon and was always beautifully styled. She made the school uniform look glamorous. When she had been questioned by the deputy headmistress as to whether or not her hair was 'peroxided', she'd told her she 'simply used Sta-Blond shampoo to bring out the natural highlights'. I knew that was a downright fib, because I used Sta-Blond shampoo and it hadn't turned my hair that shade of blonde! The final straw came when Veronica had been seen smoking and behaving in an 'undecorous' manner on the arm of an American naval officer. Veronica was allowed back into school at the start of the year to collect her belongings from the secretary's office. As a final act of defiance, when she turned up she was wearing make-up, bright red high-heeled shoes and was carrying a long umbrella with a bright red frilly cover to match. Knowing all eyes were on her, she walked confidently out of the school with her head held high, leaving in her wake a whiff of perfume which certainly hadn't come from Woolworths. We missed her for a while, she was so different.

The other piece of news at the start of the year was that Mrs Heathcote would no longer take us for Maths and Physics. She was one of our favourite teachers and we were a little sad to find out that she had left. She was the youngest and most glamorous of our teachers. She used make-up and smelled of expensive perfume. Her fingernails were the most fascinating thing about her; they were really long, beautifully manicured and painted with shiny red nail varnish. We followed her fingernails as her hand sped over the blackboard, wielding a piece of chalk, writing out equations and formulae. I think we paid more attention to her fingernails than we did to the writing on the board.

Mrs Heathcote had a very good reason for leaving the school. Her husband had been a pilot in the RAF during the war, he had been injured, although not too seriously, and he'd come home to convalesce. She had given up teaching to look after him. We thought this was so romantic.

I was lucky to have been taught by such a dedicated and superb group of women teachers. The only male teacher we had was Dr J.E. Wallace, and he taught music in a number of schools around Liverpool. In our school, on the days he came in, he played the piano at morning assembly, trained the school choir and gave each form a music lesson. He taught us to appreciate different types of music, to sight-read musical scores and encouraged us to take up a musical instrument. He also composed a school hymn.

Dr Wallace had been a student at music school with Sir Malcolm Sargent and they had remained friends. He was an excellent raconteur, his tales of what he and Malcolm Sargent – whose nickname was 'Flash Harry' – got up to as students were legendary and very amusing, and they often took up a large part of the music lesson. He introduced us to Gilbert and Sullivan, and the school productions under his direction – *The Mikado*, *Iolanthe* and *Ruddigore* – were quite outstanding. Gilbert and Sullivan operettas were not performed every year, because of the expense of paying performing rights to the D'Oyly Carte Opera Company.

Afternoon trips to the Philharmonic Hall in Liverpool were organised to listen to concerts especially put on for schools. One of the conductors was Sir Adrian Boult, who came to visit the school with a small group of players to give a talk on music and to explain how a big orchestra worked, the seating arrangements for each section of the orchestra and the difficulties they had when the orchestra had to travel with all their instruments.

What we enjoyed most about going to the concerts at the Philharmonic Hall was ogling the boys. Back then, the grammar schools were all single sex! The boys sat on one side of the auditorium and the girls sat on the other. We nipped quickly into the toilets to put on a bit of Yardley's Natural lipstick, it was very pale pink in colour and hardly noticeable, but it made us feel quite grown-up.

One of my most treasured memories of school is one day in the summer term, when I was in the fifth form, and we were sitting one of our end-of-term exams. The day was hot and the windows around the inner quadrangles were wide open. The gentle rising and falling of a humming sound came drifting through the open windows. In the hall across the quad, the senior school choir was singing the 'Humming Chorus' from Puccini's *Madame Butterfly*, practising for the end-of-term concert. It was the most beautiful music I'd ever heard. We were spellbound and stopped writing for a few moments to listen, our teacher never said a word, and then we got on with our exam. Ever since, whenever I hear the 'Humming Song' I remember that peaceful summer's day.

I took part in many activities. I couldn't sing very well and my acting wasn't too good, but art was one of my best subjects, so I worked behind the scenes, helping to paint the scenery and sew the costumes in school theatrical productions. One of the stars

of the drama group was Freda Abrahams, a tall dark Jewish girl
with a magnetic personality and a wonderful voice. I have fond
memories of her playing the lead in the production of *Androcles
and The Lion*. Freda and her family had fled to England from
Austria just before the war to escape the Nazis. Freda went on
to study medicine.

When I was old enough, I played goalkeeper in the first eleven
hockey team, and shooter in netball for the reserves. During one
netball match I tripped when aiming for the goal. I put my hand
out to save myself but only my little finger caught the goal post.
My finger cracked under the strain. The school nurse strapped
all my fingers together with a big wooden splint and placed my
arm in a sling. I had to walk home wheeling my bike. When my
mother opened the door, her first words were, 'Now what have
you done, and on a washday too.' It was Monday. She finished
the washing, made the dinner, and when my father came home
we went to the doctor's. He placed two of my fingers together in
a small splint which I would have to wear for two weeks and told
me not to bother with a sling. Next day I was back at school.

I worked in the school library as a monitor and helped to bake
cakes and make the tea for parents' evenings. I was very proud
to have been elected Form Leader three times.

Our headmistress, Miss Liddle, MA, PhD, DLitt, was about
four feet, ten inches tall and of a slight build, with pale blue eyes
and a penetrating stare. When she looked at you, you felt you
had done something wrong and would be willing to own up to
anything to avoid the merciless gaze. Her light brown hair was
neatly tucked into a navy blue ribbon.

Miss Liddle had three gowns, a plain black one, with a white
fur trim which she wore to morning assembly, another black one

with a coloured hood for seeing parents and visitors, and lastly a red gown trimmed with red satin which she wore on Speech Days and very special occasions. We knew how important each occasion was by which gown she wore.

Fidgeting and coughing were forbidden in morning assembly, and excuses would not be tolerated. All that was necessary to stop a cough, said Miss Liddle, was a good hard swallow. In the winter, looking round the hall it was easy to see people swallowing and going red in the face as they tried desperately hard to stop a cough from bursting out. Anyone who coughed had to line up after assembly and apologise to Miss Liddle for the interruption.

When a member of staff was off for any reason, Miss Liddle would come and take the lesson. When she gave us a poem or a piece from the Bible to learn, we made sure we were absolutely word perfect. During the lesson she would walk around stopping at a desk here and there to say 'Tie that hair back', 'Cut your hair' and sometimes, lifting a lock up between her thumb and forefinger, she would say, 'Wash this hair!'

Miss Liddle took the opportunity to tell us how important good deportment was to our future well-being. We had to walk tall, sit up straight and never slouch over the desk, even when we were writing. This would ensure that we would not have back trouble in later life, or suffer from digestion problems as our stomachs would never be scrunched up. Teachers had to observe pupils and keep a record of those who had good posture at all times, particularly in lessons. At the end of each year, posture stripes were awarded. They were small silver strips sewn onto navy blue ribbon, which we pinned onto our school pullovers or blouses. I managed to achieve three stripes and became a posture 'sergeant'.

Normally, we had to use the rear and side doors at either end of the school building. Pupils were not allowed to use the front doorway, except at the end of each term, when Miss Liddle would stand in the doorway at the main entrance and everyone had to line up for her to shake our hand and wish each one of us a 'Happy holiday'. This ceremony took quite a long time, as nearly 700 pupils in the school filed out one by one. Miss Liddle must have had a phenomenal memory because she knew everyone by name. Woe betide anyone who tried to sneak out the back door to get away quickly; she would know who was missing, and at the beginning of the next term they would be put on detention.

The intake each year was 100 girls, who would be split up into three forms, A, B and C. We were taught in our forms for most lessons, but for Maths and French we were divided into four groups according to ability – Alpha, Beta, Gamma and Delta. I was in Alpha Maths and Beta French. I found Maths easy and enjoyable. At the end of our five years' schooling we all had to sit the same final exam, the School Certificate, taking a minimum of seven subjects. Pupils' weaknesses were carefully monitored and extra help was given where necessary. Most girls took more than seven subjects; I sat nine subjects and passed them all. If anyone failed a subject they had to retake the whole year, so it was important to make sure that any weaknesses in Maths and Languages were ironed out before the exams were taken. Smaller groups meant more individual attention.

In the late 1930s, the school had moved from old cramped premises in the city to a new building on the outskirts, with good modern facilities and playing fields just a short walk away. When we arrived at school each morning, we took our coats and hats off and changed our shoes in the cloakroom. The cloakroom had quarry tile floors, with long benches down the centre. We removed our outdoor shoes, put them in the wire baskets beneath the benches then put on the indoor shoes we had to wear, in order to protect the parquet wood floors in the main part of the school. The indoor shoes were all regulation issue with fine leather soles, soft black leather uppers and a single strap across the instep, held in place by a button.

Although sliding on the polished floors was forbidden, with a good run-up it was possible, even in our soft indoor shoes. I knew, because one afternoon, with no one around, I was in the middle of a really good slide along the corridor when I crashed into Miss Liddle who was coming round the corner. I got lines and detention!

Miss McMeckan, our chemistry teacher, was quite old and should have retired, but she had stayed on during the war because of the shortage of science teachers. She was more than a little eccentric.

As well as teaching chemistry, she was the lost property mistress. On the side of her bench at the front of the lab, she kept a large wicker basket containing all the lost property, everything except valuable items like purses, fountain pens and watches. They were kept in the secretary's office. Suddenly, for no apparent reason, in the middle of a chemistry lesson she would root in the basket and come up with an item of clothing, usually underwear, such as a bra or a pair of knickers. She would hold up the item and shout out, 'Who does this belong to?' I never saw anyone claim anything and I'm not surprised, we were too embarrassed. I wondered how someone could go home without their knickers or bra. My mother would have known if anything of mine was missing from the wash. At the end of each term, all unclaimed items were washed, laid out on display, then sold; the money went into school funds.

One year, we were taken for English by Miss Rabson. We had not met her before because she was the senior English mistress who taught the sixth form. An Oxford graduate, as many of our teachers were, she was a good teacher and very clever. One unusual thing about her was her left eye, which didn't move when the other one did. At the start of the first lesson, Miss Rabson called out our names and we had to stand up so she could match the name to the face and make a mental note of who we were. She read out the first name of each girl in turn. When she said: 'Doris, stand up', this was a problem. There were two girls in the form called Doris, me and Doris Lee. We both stood up. We were sitting on opposite sides of the room to avoid confusion. I realised what had happened. Because of Miss Rabson's lazy eye, we didn't know which Doris she was talking to.

There are times when instinct tells you not to do anything but keep absolutely still. This was one of them. I stared straight ahead, as did the other Doris, we didn't dare look at each other and neither of us made any attempt to sit down. I held my breath, and there was a tense silence in the room. Miss Rabson stared at everyone for a few seconds then asked loudly and slowly, 'Do you think I am cross-eyed?' At this, the rest of the form exploded with laughter, while we stood and waited for the laughter to die down, not moving a muscle. The whole form was put on detention. Somehow, Miss Rabson had the idea that I was responsible for this incident, although for the life of me I could not see what I had done wrong.

For the rest of the year, whenever a piece of homework had to be learnt by heart, such as a poem or a long speech from Shakespeare, she made sure that I was the one who had to stand up and recite it, and she marked my essays very critically indeed.

Good clear writing was considered essential and we had to write with a fountain pen. Our names had to be engraved on our pens, and to make sure we wrote well Miss Abbott, the geography teacher, turned some of her lessons into calligraphy exercises. On the blackboard she wrote out the letters of the alphabet showing us how join our writing to keep it flowing smoothly. We would go through the letters of the alphabet very carefully writing out two lines of each letter: aaaaaa, bbbbbb, cccccc and so on right through the alphabet. When we'd finished, Miss Abbott dictated some unusual words with difficult letter patterns for more practise. Our notebooks were a pleasure to look at.

School dinners were cooked on the premises and were pretty good. We were not allowed out of school at lunchtime and there were no packed lunches, dinner was compulsory. At the beginning of each week we paid 2/6 for five dinner tickets. Because of the number of girls in school there were two lunch sittings. The regulation navy blue school knickers that we wore had to have a pocket for our dinner tickets. To a stranger it must have looked very funny to see over 300 hungry girls walking as quickly as possible down the corridor to the dining room, all fumbling in their knickers for their dinner tickets. And not too hygienic either!

We sat at tables of ten, five down each side, with a senior girl as server at the head of each table. She served out the food from a large dish that had been brought to the table. Before we ate, we stood still with our heads bowed and said grace: 'For what we are about to receive, may the Lord make us truly thankful.' When we'd finished eating and the tables were cleared, we stood again to say 'Thank you Lord, for what we have received. Amen'. When Miss Brunelle, the French Mistress who had come from Paris to teach French, was on dinner duty, at the end of the prayer instead of Amen we said 'Ainsi soit-il'.

Miss Brunelle was small thin and wiry, straight up and down with bright black eyes in a pinched face and shiny black hair drawn severely back in a bun. Her clothes were still in the style of the 1920s: a long straight skirt, with a long belted jacket. She was a strict disciplinarian and a stickler for the school rules. Rules about school uniform had to be strictly observed. Hats had to be worn with our uniform at all times when travelling back and forth to school. One day, cycling home from school, my velour hat slipped off my head and was held on round my neck with a piece of elastic. I suddenly had the feeling I was being watched. A tramway ran along the centre of the dual carriageway. I looked to my right and there sitting on a tram coming alongside me was Miss Brunelle. She lifted her forefinger, pointing it at me as the tram went by. I thought to myself, she can't do anything to me, she's on the tram. How wrong I was! Two stops later she got off the tram and was standing in the middle of the road waiting for me. As I approached, she held up her hand and said in a loud voice: 'Arrêtez-vous!' When I stopped in front of her, she said, 'Your hat is not on your head.' She wrote down my name and form, and I was reported to my form mistress and given lines and a detention.

When I complained to my mother about being given a detention, for the hat incident or anything else, I never got any sympathy from her; she would say it's your own fault for not obeying the rules.

A girl in our form whose French was equal to that of Miss Brunelle was Ruth de Gruchy. Her home was in the Channel Islands. She and her family were staying with relatives in England. They had managed to escape in a small boat just before the Germans invaded the Channel Islands and they planned to return once the war was over. It never occurred to us that we would lose the war; it was just a question of when we would win. Ruth was always so pleasant. We found it difficult to believe that the family had to abandon their home and all their belongings; we were suffering some discomfort but nothing quite so devastating.

For the first three years, each term we did Biology then Chemistry then Physics, before we opted for the sciences we wanted to do in the final two years and take in the final exam. The last Biology session was reproduction. We started with frogspawn and tadpoles, then onto birds and bees, gradually working our way up to human beings. At the end of the course a lady doctor came in to talk to us and answer any questions we might have. Only a very brave person would have put their hand up. Although up to this point we knew where babies came from and we thought we knew how they were conceived, when it was finally confirmed and explained in detail, we were shocked and disgusted to find out what our parents had done to produce us.

My father was interested in my homework and liked to check to make sure I had completed everything. He listened as I recited my learning homework, such as speeches and poetry for English, and theorems for Maths. For the next Biology homework in my science exercise book I had to draw the male and female reproductive organs from diagrams that we'd been given. I was horrified and went to tremendous lengths to hide my book in case he saw what I was doing!

History was such an interesting subject and one that I really enjoyed. Our teacher, Miss Attlee, had short silver hair and was so enthusiastic that she passed her love of the subject on to us. Miss Attlee taught us not to take things at face value, to gather all the facts and think for ourselves. There was often a rational explanation for something which could be deemed a miracle.

For example, in the Bible, the crossing of the river Jordan by the Israelites could be explained away because it may have been an unusual tide that left the river bed dry. When a woman who appeared to be a cripple was ordered by Jesus to get up and walk and she did so, the illness could have been psychosomatic. From an early age Jesus had sat in the back of the temple listening to the wise men talking and he would have learnt so many things. He would have known about the eclipses of the sun and the moon and when they would take place. When he told the people he would make the world dark this was probably what he was talking about. After the war, Miss Attlee went on to lecture at a teacher training college.

When I went home and told my mother about the interesting things we had discussed, she was not too happy and thought they might be too controversial. My father, on the other hand, who was a very intelligent man, was keen to talk through these ideas with me.

At the end of every school year, Miss Liddle gave a talk on careers. She was concerned that our education should not be wasted. She said we were all capable of reaching our full potential because of the schooling we had been given, and she encouraged us to go into one of the professions if it was possible. The one thing she did not approve of was 'shorthand and typing' – the mere mention of this occupation was enough to make her lips curl in contempt.

I didn't see much of Mary when I was in school because she was in a different form. I had three good friends in my form, Barbara, Brenda and Doreen. Barbara was my best friend. We loved tennis and played every time we got a chance, not only in school but outside too. Barbara belonged to a private tennis club and used to take me as a visitor. My mother once said to me, 'The only time I see you is when you come home to whiten your pumps.' We also went ice-skating together, as Barbara also had her own skates. We learnt to do a waltz. Barbara decided on a career in scientific research and when she qualified, she went off to live in Australia. Brenda married a lieutenant in the South African Navy. Doreen also went abroad.

Another friend I had was Joan. She was in a different form and our mothers were good friends. In the summer after the war, Joan's mother was going into hospital for a small operation and would be in for a few days. Joan's father owned and ran a grocer's shop and could not afford to close it, so Joan was going to stay with her auntie who was housekeeper to the people who owned a well-known shipping line. Joan's mother thought it would be a good idea if I went too, to keep Joan company. Joan's father arrived in his Morris Eight to pick me up. When we arrived at the house I was very impressed, it was a large detached double-fronted Victorian villa, with steps up to the front door. We went in round the back, where there was a notice in large letters, saying 'Tradesman's Entrance'.

I had never been in such a grand house. The family had gone away for the first time in many years, leaving Joan's aunt in charge as the house was being decorated and refurbished. The furniture in the main rooms of the house was covered in dust sheets and all the precious ornaments had been put in store. We were allowed to wander round the house as long as we behaved ourselves, didn't touch anything, kept out of the private family rooms and didn't disturb the workmen, who were very busy. We were to sleep in a room at the top of the house usually occupied by one of the servants.

The two things that impressed me the most were the Grand Piano and the library. The piano was very shiny and black, draped with a beautiful cream silk Spanish shawl embroidered with brilliant flowers. The library was full of books about people and things I'd never heard of. We were allowed to choose a book to take out into the garden to read. It was a lovely summer's day and we sat on wicker chairs at a wicker table and had tea and homemade cakes, brought out to us on a tray by Joan's auntie; we felt like little ladies. I think she was glad to have us in the house as company for a few days. It must have been quite lonely in that big house after the workmen had gone home.

After a lot of browsing, the book I'd picked was about yoga. As I turned the pages I was astonished – I never knew such a thing existed! The art and the mystical meanings of yoga were explained and the pictures of wise Indian men twisting themselves into unbelievable positions were stunning. Instructions on how to swallow your own tongue were shown. The most startling illustrations I found were the ones showing Indian fakirs wearing only a loincloth, lying on beds of nails! A question of mind over matter. Joan and I spent some time rolling around the lawn in fits of laughter as we tried to imitate some of the positions. In the end we gave up, it was a warm sunny day and we had other things to do.

It was a memorable few days. I couldn't wait to get home and tell my parents about the house and everything I'd seen. My mother was interested in the household things and the pantry, but I knew my father would be interested to hear about the books in the library, the one on yoga in particular.

❖❖❖

I was quite sorry when I had to leave school, I think we all were. As we said our tearful farewells we made promises to keep in touch, but we went our separate ways and most of us never did. We were quite widely dispersed as we followed our different careers, some even went abroad. What we took with us was such a good feeling of friendship and pride in belonging to 'our school'.

Many years after I left, I met an old school friend whose husband was working in the management side of education. He had met Miss Liddle who, although she had retired from teaching, was now working as an education adviser. He could not understand how we could possibly have been afraid of such a charming old lady!

In September 1948, after a good summer holiday, I was to start work in the Liver Buildings in the Treasury Department of a major insurance company. My days of skipping and cycling to school were over.

If you enjoyed this book, you may also be interested in …

Liverpool's Children in the 1950s
PAMELA RUSSELL

This book is packed with the experience of schooldays, holidays, games, clubs and hobbies of a bygone era. As the decade progressed, rationing ended and children's pocket money was spent on goodies like Chocstix, Spangles, Wagon Wheels and Fry's Five Boys. This book opens a window on an exciting period of optimism, when anything seemed possible, described by the children and teenagers who experienced it.

978 0 7524 5901 1

Liverpool Then & Now
DANIEL K. LONGMAN

The popular tourist city of Liverpool has a rich heritage, which is uniquely reflected in this fascinating new compilation. Contrasting a selection of forty-five archive images alongside full-colour modern photographs, this book delves into the changing faces and buildings of Liverpool.

978 0 7524 5740 6

Liverpool's Children in the Second World War
PAMELA RUSSELL

This is the untold story of Liverpool's children in the Second World War. Whilst everyone is familiar with the tales of evacuees who were rushed out of the cities once the bombs started falling, many of us are unaware that many stayed behind, either by choice or necessity, as the city of their childhood disintegrated and burned around them. In the words of those who experienced the Liverpool Blitz first-hand, we hear of their adventures and misadventures, the ever-present danger, and the humour and sorrow of those wartime years.

978 0 7524 5158 9

Visit our website and discover thousands of other History Press books.

www.thehistorypress.co.uk